ATE:

AUTOMATIC
TEST EQUIPMENT

ATE:
AUTOMATIC
TEST EQUIPMENT

ALLAN C. STOVER, B.S.E.E., M.S., P.E.

Senior Engineer, Westinghouse Electric Corporation

McGRAW-HILL BOOK COMPANY
New York   St. Louis   San Francisco   Auckland   Bogotá
Hamburg   Johannesburg   London   Madrid   Mexico
Montreal   New Delhi   Panama   Paris   São Paulo
Singapore   Sydney   Tokyo   Toronto

Library of Congress Cataloging in Publication Data

Stover, Allan C.
  ATE: automatic test equipment.

  Index included.
  1. Automatic checkout equipment.   I. Title.
II. Title: A.T.E.
TK7895.A8S86   1984   621.3815′48   83-14917
ISBN 0-07-061792-9

1234567890   DOC/DOC   89876543

ISBN 0-07-061792-9

The editors for this book were Harry Helms and Stephan O. Parnes, the designer was Elliot Epstein, and the production supervisor was Teresa F. Leaden. It was set in Caledonia by Waldman Graphics, Inc.,

Printed and bound by R. R. Donnelley & Sons Company

To Liz, Grace, and Natalie

CONTENTS

PREFACE

The field of automatic test equipment (ATE) is a vast one, with scores of variations in systems, hardware, and software. Even those who have worked in the field for some years may find the subject overwhelming at times, especially in light of recent progress and challenges.

When I tried to find a textbook on ATE some time ago, however, I found few available, none of them recent. I realized that a need existed for a book that would tie everything together, with material of interest to the wide technical audience that is associated in some way with ATE.

I aimed this book at those associated with ATE, such as test engineers, technicians, managers, and support, marketing, reliability, and quality assurance personnel, as well as those in the ATE field, such as engineers, supervisors, and programmers. I felt the book should also be of use to those who simply want to learn more about the expanding ATE field. I therefore tried to make the discussions as thorough as possible.

Because of the complex relationship that exists between hardware and software in ATE systems, I have covered both. I have devoted some chapters to one or the other, while other chapters contain some of both in order to tie them together.

I have also been interested for some time in the potential reliability problems that can result from the speed of ATE systems and the lack of human control over the test cycle. Although ATE systems are probably a factor more reliable than manual methods, they harbor the potential for subtle reliability problems in hardware and software. I have therefore discussed some potential problems and solutions.

In order to relate the discussions to the "real world," I have covered a number of ATE systems, controllers, instruments, and other related products. I have selected the examples to cover as broadly as possible the equipment that is used today. A careful reading of the specifications and capabilities should prove useful. I have tried to present each product objectively, while pointing out the features I felt related to the discussion. My selection of a particular product is not in any way meant as an endorsement. I chose them as representative examples.

I have drawn on the talents of a number of people who have reviewd the text, provided information, or helped in some way to make the book broader in scope or more accurate. I cannot take the space to thank everyone and I hope that those I missed will understand. I am especially grateful to Kristin Baraniak, GenRad, Inc.; Richard Harmone and Orion Wood, Hewlett-Packard Company; Ron Gerst, Fluke Automated Systems; Norbert Laengrich, Racal Dana Instruments, Inc.; Debi Tokarczyk, Bendix; Paul Birman, Kepco, Inc.; David Van Cleve, Data General; Larry Van Horn, Fairchild; Marty Taucher, John Fluke Mfg. Co.; G. K. Mercola, ICS Electronics Corp.; Ronald Robinson, Everett/Charles Contact Products, Inc.; Mary Harmon, Keithley Instruments, Inc.; Dave Hiltner, Zehntel; J. P. Stowers, Virginia Panel Corp.; Diana Wade, Tektronix, Inc.; and R. E. Hightower, Wavetek. I am also grateful to Intel Corp.; Marconi Instruments; Systron Donner; Instrumentation Engineering; EML Automation, Inc.; Autek Systems Corp.; Julie Research Laboratories, Inc.; Digital Equipment Corp.; Ziatech Corp.; and Teradyne, Inc.

I also thank those at Westinghouse, including Cobey Kaufman, Dennis Wiens, Gary Moffitt, Jay Koontz, and Jack Wright. I am also grateful to Kathy Surkovich and Kathy Gately for their help.

Allan C. Stover

ATE:

AUTOMATIC
TEST EQUIPMENT

1

A REVIEW
OF ATE

Automation has swept the electronics industry. Computers now handle the design and manufacture of printed circuit boards that make up the electronic assemblies and equipment. Small wonder, then, that the electronics industry has also automated the testing of those boards, assemblies, and equipment through the use of automatic test equipment (ATE).

Organizations that have switched over to automated testing have experienced a number of benefits. Few developments have improved product quality and productivity in the electronics industry as much as ATE. ATE runs tests in a fraction of the time needed by a manual test set, where the technician performs the interconnections, adjustments, and measurements and records the results by hand. An operator with a minimum of training can perform complex tests with ATE. In some instances, the UUT (unit under test) specifications are so complex and the data requirements so vast that only ATE will handle them.

ATE also contributes to an improvement in product quality through the transfer of control over the test cycle from an operator to an electronic controller. Test departments can thus minimize the errors, omissions, faulty judgments, erroneous measurements, and other such drawbacks of human control. This benefit can result in a shorter payback period for ATE, especially since the cost of correcting errors and faults can increase manyfold at each level they are missed. In addition, ATE eliminates many repetitious and tedious steps from tests, which leaves only the steps that require human judgment and involvement. This benefit improves the quality of the work environment for test personnel.

IN THE BEGINNING

Electronics companies have tested their products in some way since the early days of radio. To test a radio in the early days, a radio engineer may have simply tuned in to a nearby radio station to check the reception.

As radios and electronics equipment grew more complex and test equipment developed into more useful forms, organizations began to rely more and more on "electronics to test electronics." Over the years, test benches multiplied as fast as the electronics field expanded. Meters, oscillators, and oscilloscopes cluttered the benches. Technicians fetched the UUT, applied power, hooked up cables between UUT test points and the test equipment, set the dials, threw the switches, made the measurements, recorded the results, and struggled through a step-by-step test procedure that sometimes took hours or even days to complete. Overall, the test-bench method wasted much of the technician's time. Organizations still find their test benches economical to use, but primarily for such uses as the testing of low-production items.

MANUAL TEST SETS

A few decades ago, engineers took a hard look at testing and concluded that the test-bench method was too inefficient for high-volume production testing. They gathered all of the test equipment for a UUT or group of UUTs together into a single console, often with a switching, interconnection, and control panel to simplify connections. Technicians still had to hook up cables to the UUT, set the dials, make the measurements, and record the results, but they tested UUTs faster because everything they needed was stacked up in front of them and they made the interconnections faster. Fig. 1-1 shows a manual test set layout.

Since the manual method relies on human control, however, it (as the test-bench method) is still plagued with human errors. Technicians may set dials in error, misinterpret readings, read the wrong scales, and set up test equipment incorrectly. When they are fatigued, confused, or upset, their productivity and the quality of their work suffer.

THE NEXT STEP: AUTOMATED TESTING

The next logical step along the way removed much of the human control over routine steps and automated the test cycle. Fig. 1-2 shows a simplified block diagram of ATE that emphasizes the basic components. Fig. 1-3 shows a block diagram of Instrumentation Engineering 390 Automatic Analog/Digital/Hybrid Test system. ATE systems vary considerably and it is difficult to generalize, but most contain the following items in some form:

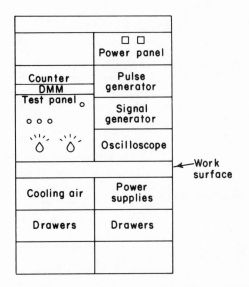

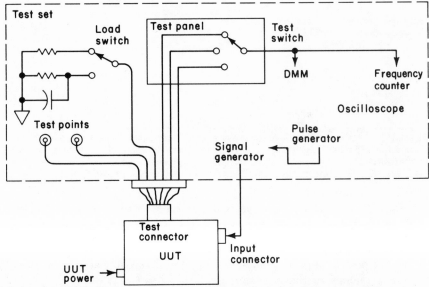

Fig. 1-1 Layout of a typical manual test set. The test equipment provides the UUT inputs and reads the signal values at the UUT test points. The entire operation is under the control of a test technician.

1. A *controller* (generally a minicomputer, microcomputer, calculator, or dedicated bus controller) that manages the test cycle, controls the flow of data, receives measurement results, processes the data, checks whether the readings are within tolerance, performs calculations, and outputs the

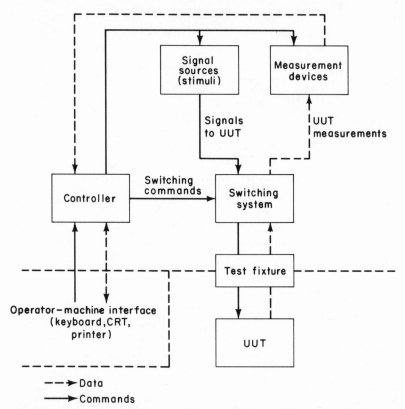

Fig. 1-2 Layout of an ATE system. The signal sources (stimuli) provide input signals to the UUT. The measuring devices measure signals at the UUT. The switching system routes the signals. The controller controls the test cycle and processes the data. The controller can be a calculator, computer, or microprocessor circuit, among other possibilities. The operator-machine interface may or may not be part of the controller.

results to a display or printer. The controller requires software in the form of a test program to control each step in the test cycle.

2. *Stimuli,* or signal sources, that provide input signals to the UUT. They may be power supplies, a function generator, digital-to-analog converters, or a frequency synthesizer, among others.

3. *Measuring instruments* that measure the UUT output signals. They can be analog-to-digital converters, frequency counters, digital multimeters, or any other type of measuring device.

4. A *switching system* that routes the signals between the UUT and other items in the ATE system.

5. An *operator-machine interface* for two-way communication between the controller and the operator. This interface may be part of the controller.

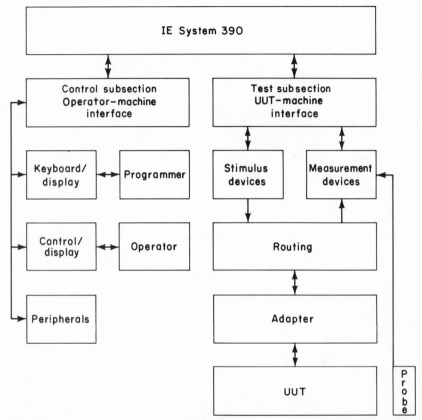

Fig. 1-3 Block diagram of Instrumentation Engineering 390 Automatic Test System. The controller, operator-machine interface, stimuli (stimulus devices), measuring devices, switching system (routing), and fixture (adapter) are parts of most ATE systems. *(Courtesy Instrumentation Engineering, Inc.)*

It may also take the form of switches, lights, and displays on a control console. Most often, the operator inputs information to the controller by means of a keyboard or switches. The controller outputs information, results, and requests for operator action to a cathode ray tube (CRT), light-emitting diode (LED) display, or set of lights. It outputs test results to a printer if a hard copy is required.

6. A UUT-machine interface through the test circuitry and fixture.

Fig. 1-4 shows a more detailed layout for one type of ATE. The function generator provides input signals to the UUT. The frequency counter and digital multimeter (DMM) make measurements at UUT test points. The DMM can take readings of ac or dc signal levels at various test points, or it can measure the resistance of UUT components connected across test

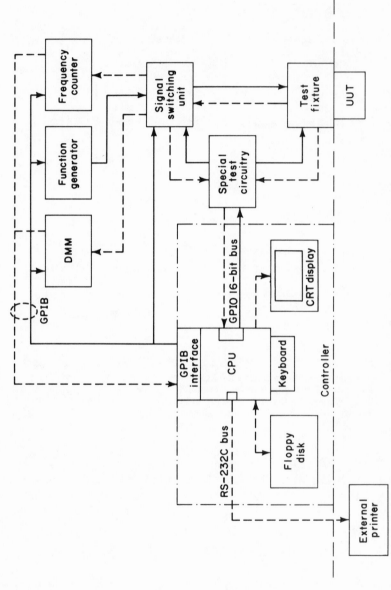

Fig. 1-4 Layout of an ATE system. The function generator provides inputs to the UUT, and the DMM and frequency counter measure the outputs. The switching system interconnects the test equipment, UUT interfaces, and the special test circuitry. The controller contains a CRT display, keyboard, and floppy disk. It sends test data over the RS-232C bus to an external printer and communicates with special test circuits over a 16-bit parallel bus.

6

points. The controller here is an electronic calculator that contains a floppy disk for the test program, a CRT display, a keyboard, special function keys, and a small printer. The display provides information and requests to the operator, while the printer provides a hard copy of the test results.

The controller generally communicates with the switching unit, stimuli, and measuring instruments over a 16-line bus, commonly called the general purpose interface bus (GPIB) or IEEE-488 bus, since the Institute of Electrical and Electronics Engineers (IEEE) published a bus standard in 1975. It is also called the IEC bus because the International Electrotechnical Commission joined with IEEE in standardizing the bus worldwide. Hewlett-Packard, which supplies many calculator-controllers and GPIB instruments, calls its version HP-IB, or Hewlett-Packard Interface Bus. Commands from the controller and readings from the measuring instruments pass over the GPIB. Many manufacturers of test equipment offer an "IEEE-488 option" or "GPIB version" that allows their product to be used under GPIB control. This text will use the terms IEEE-488 and GPIB interchangeably.

Although the GPIB is extensively used in ATE, other serial and parallel buses are used. The controller may use its own bus for the peripherals. Many manufacturers use their own bus design inside their ATE.

THE ATE TEST CYCLE

It may be instructive to review a test cycle for the ATE in Fig. 1-4 in some detail. Assume that the operator has loaded the program into the controller memory by means of a floppy disk. After entry of some preliminary information, such as the UUT model number (so the controller will call up the appropriate test program) and the UUT serial number and date (for the test result printout), the controller enters the first test cycle. Assume that in this portion of the test, the ATE system must output a 26-V 400-Hz sine wave reference signal to an input pin at the UUT connector, then read a resulting frequency and ac voltage at a UUT test point. The ATE will go through the following steps under control of the ATE software, although the actual order could vary somewhat:

1. Over the GPIB, the controller sends the commands that set up the function generator to provide a 26-V 400-Hz sine wave signal. The function generator responds with the commanded signal.

2. The controller then commands the switching unit to connect the function generator output to the UUT input. The switching unit makes the correct connection.

3. The controller commands the switching unit to connect the selected UUT test point to the DMM input. The switching unit makes the connection.

It should be noted that a number of off-the-shelf switching systems have the ability to make only one interconnection at a time. If such a system were used in the example ATE system, the connections in steps 2 and 3 above would require a second switching system or another method of connecting either the input signal or the output connection to the DMM.

4. The controller sends the commands that set up the DMM to measure ac voltage. The DMM enters the commanded mode (AC VOLTS).

5. The controller commands the DMM to read the ac voltage at its input and send that value in digital form over the GPIB for input to the controller. The DMM responds and sends the signal over the bus.

6. The controller reads the value of ac voltage sent by the DMM.

7. The controller commands the switching unit to connect the frequency counter input to the UUT test point. The switching unit makes the connection.

8. The controller sends the commands that set up the frequency counter to measure the frequency at its input. The frequency counter enters the commanded mode (FREQUENCY MEASUREMENT).

9. The controller commands the frequency counter to read the frequency of the signal at its input and send that value over the GPIB. The frequency counter responds and places the value on the GPIB.

10. The controller reads in the value of frequency from the bus.

11. The controller computes whether the voltage and frequency are within tolerance, then prints out pass or fail depending on the results.

12. The controller program continues on to the next test.

The above is a simple step-by-step procedure. It is presented in this manner to illustrate the detail to which the programmer must go to write the test program. The ATE can go through the whole cycle in seconds, whereas a technician on a test bench could take minutes for each test and within a short time grow bored with the repetitive measurements.

THE TYPES OF ATE

A number of ATE systems are available today, and one can be found or constructed in-house to fit almost any testing situation. Off-the-shelf ATE systems are available from a number of manufacturers. One should perform a thorough study of the requirements and the systems available before a purchase is made.

Any definition of ATE should include all of the possible variations in the automated testing of products. As we will see, the variations are extensive. Most systems, however, fall into one of five categories:

• In-circuit

• Functional

• Known-good system

• Comparison

• Semiconductors and components

The following discussion covers some highlights of each ATE category.

In-Circuit Test Systems

The in-circuit test system (ICT) tests printed circuit boards for such parameters as continuity, short circuits, and open circuits, and measures and tests the devices on assembled boards. As a result, ICTs may check bare boards or assembled boards or both. It has been estimated that ICTs isolate up to 98 percent of common board defects, although the actual percentage would depend on a number of factors.

Generally, the board is placed onto a "bed-of-nails" fixture (see Fig. 1-5) that contains a number of spring-loaded pins (sometimes over 3000) that make contact at desired points on the board. A vacuum, pneumatic, or manual system presses the board and pins together for a good contact. The ICT may require a different fixture configuration for each board.

The fixture pins generally connect to drivers and sensors so measurements on digital ICs (integrated circuits) can be made at each pin. The test patterns may follow a Gray code format or other pattern that will exercise a number of input combinations. The ICT can force the inputs to a particular state and then sense the state of the outputs. Some ICTs have random access memory (RAM) at each pin to keep up with the high test pattern rates for dynamic testing.

Upon receiving a start command from the operator, the controller (often a minicomputer with a disk memory) commands the ICT instrumentation to measure the various parameters at each point. It may test the board first for open circuits, short circuits, and continuity, then perform static or dynamic tests on digital ICs. If it contains analog instrumentation, it can also test analog components, such as resistors, capacitors, inductors, diodes, op-amps, and transistors.

Fig. 1-5 Bed-of-nails fixture for an ATE system with a circuit board being inserted for testing. *(Courtesy of Hewlett-Packard Company.)*

A software device library on the ICT disk memory contains the characteristics of a number of components. ICT memory will also contain a map generated from user-provided information with the location and type of each device on the board. The ICT will isolate one device at a time, apply the proper signal, make the appropriate measurement, then compare the output values with the limits contained in the device library. The ICT is therefore quite useful in locating short circuits, open circuits, and components that are defective, incorrect, missing, or misinstalled. The idea behind the ICT is that the board must be good if each track and component is tested and found to be good.

Functional Test System

A functional tester performs its tests on a UUT (board, assembly, system, etc.) by applying various stimuli at the UUT inputs, then measuring the resulting UUT response. With a printed circuit board, for example, the tester might apply power and a test signal at the power and signal input pins of the UUT edge connector. It will measure the response of the circuitry at the output pins of the connector and compare the results with the expected response in the tester memory.

The functional tester generally uses one of two methods to check the response of the UUT to the stimuli: stored response and signature analysis. With stored response, an actual bit pattern is stored in memory for direct comparison with the UUT response. Signature analysis, a data compression technique that requires less memory, will be discussed in a later chapter. It should be noted that these responses can be read at the UUT connector or be measured at various points by the operator using a probe and guided by instructions from the tester's software.

Known-Good System ("Hot Mock-up")

With this tester, an entire end product is maintained at the ATE system. The operator removes a good unit from the system and inserts the UUT. Test signals are applied to the system and the responses noted. If the system passes the test, the UUT is assumed to be good.

This method is generally more economical than other ATE, but the test may miss subtle faults buried in the unit under test. The UUT may work only with that particular system but fail in any other system into which it is placed. This ATE system seldom has any provisions to aid in fault isolation if a system fails. This method has been used with success in small production runs where the cost of more conventional ATE would be prohibitive.

Comparison Test System

The comparison tester compares the UUT with a reference unit known to be good. The tester applies the same signals to both units simultaneously, then compares the responses at the outputs or other nodes. If the responses differ, the tester can guide the operator to the fault using a guided-probe technique. By comparing each test point on the reference unit with the UUT, the comparison tester eliminates the need to maintain a large memory of reference data. The reference board serves as a store of responses to the various stimuli.

The comparison tester represents an economical method of testing UUTs. The idea behind the comparison tester is that the UUT must be good if it and the reference board have identical responses to various stimuli.

Semiconductor and Component Test Systems

The semiconductor and component test category includes a wide range of ATE systems that test individual components. Some test digital devices, including VLSI (very large scale integrated) circuits, memory chips, and microprocessors. Others specialize in analog devices. Some test discrete semiconductors, such as transistors, diodes, and zener diodes. Still others test such components as resistors or capacitors at high speed. Some specialize in one type of device within its group while others test a few different types.

The requirements within this category vary considerably. A test system for RAM chips, for example, must have the ability to provide complex test patterns in order to test the chip's memory locations and control pins. A resistor test system, on the other hand, measures single values of resistance, and its complexity is relatively low. The production rate of the resistor tester, however, would probably run many times higher than that of the RAM tester.

TODAY'S ATE

A number of ATE systems are available on the market today. They vary considerably in their layout and capabilities. Some fit well into one of the five categories, while others fit in two or three or none at all. Because of the expanding need for ATE, a number of companies have entered the market. Many other companies manufacture their own systems because they can custom build them to suit specific needs. Some of these companies also custom build ATE for their customers.

Some ATE systems today are fully automatic. They require an operator only to load and remove UUTs and press a button or two. Other ATE systems are semiautomatic and require a technician to adjust the signals and make the measurements. From this large inventory, a few representative types have been selected for presentation.

Fluke Automated Systems 3050B Digital/Analog Test System

The 3050B, shown in Fig. 1-6, is an example of a comparison tester. It can test and aid in the troubleshooting of SSI (small-scale integrated), MSI (medium-scale integrated) and LSI (large-scale integrated) circuit boards and

Fig. 1-6 Fluke 3050B Digital/Analog Test System, a reference board comparison system. At the right is the main test console. To its left is the 3053A Analog Test Station, which houses stimuli and measurement devices. Further to the left is the 3051B Offline Programming station and printer for offline program generation and documentation. *(Courtesy of Fluke Automated Systems.)*

multibus boards with self-clock microprocessors. To determine the board faults, the 3050B applies identical signals to the edge connectors on both a reference board and the board under test.

Although comparison testers normally require less memory than the incircuit and functional test systems (the reference board serves as the "data storage" of acceptable signals at each node), the 3050B contains an extensive software system. Its Test Management System aids in the control of test and diagnostic routines. It also contains an Automatic Fault Emulator that checks the quality of the test program. The automatic fault diagnostics software provides printed circuit board diagnostics with guided probe and clip.

Fluke offers a number of options with the 3050B. The 3051B Programming Station allows a programmer to prepare test and diagnostic programs offline. An RS-232 cable can be used to connect it to the 3050B to debug and modify programs online, even during a test.

The 3053A IEEE-488 Instrument Module allows the user to expand the 3050B with test equipment that has IEEE-488 bus capability. The 3053A allows the user to measure such parameters as timing, frequency, voltage, resistance, and capacitance.

Genrad 1796 Functional Test System

The 1796 is a functional ATE system that tests digital, analog, and hybrid printed circuit boards and detects faults down to the component level. Each pin of the 1796 contains 4K bits of RAM and a digital driver/sensor that is individually programmable to ± 30 V.

The 1796 also contains the following analog stimulus and measurement modules for the functional testing of analog and hybrid boards:

Stimuli Ac signal sources furnish sine, square, and rectangular waveforms at frequencies up to 10 MHz. A pulse generator is programmable in pulse amplitude, duration, rise and fall time, and number of transistions.

Measurement An ac measurement unit contains the ability to measure ac characteristics from 50 Hz to 7 MHz. A dc measurement unit makes dc differential voltage and current measurements. A resistance measurement unit provides 4-terminal kelvin or guarded resistance measurements from 0 to 10 MΩ. A frequency measurement unit measures frequency, period, multiple period, frequency ratio, and time interval. The frequency capability ranges from 0.012 Hz to 40 MHz. Time interval measurements run from 2 ns (nanoseconds) to 1.6 s.

An optional four-phase clock generator allows the controller to program each clock input for a frequency of up to 20 MHz with as many as 32 clock transitions. The clock generator provides overlapping waveforms for multiphase clock synchronization between the clock generator, test system, and UUT.

Fig. 1-7 GenRad 1796 Digital/Analog Test System. The CRT data terminal and keyboard for program preparation and diagnostic probe sequences is at the left. The test system control panel for operator interface is next to it. To the right is the diagnostic resolution module with a 40-pin IC clip and current-injecting microvoltmeter probe. *(Courtesy of GenRad, Inc., Concord, Mass.)*

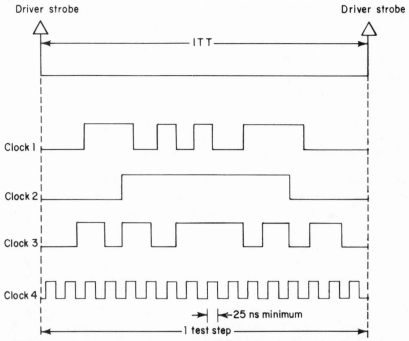

Fig. 1-8 1796 Clock generator signals. Each of four clock signals can be independently programmed with 1796 software. *(Courtesy of GenRad, Inc., Concord, Mass.)*

The 1796 software is simulator-based, in that it simulates in software the circuit to be tested. With some training, a typist can enter the required schematic data into the 1796. The test engineer will then work with the interactive software to develop the test programs for one segment of the board at a time. This segmentation of the board is a recommended procedure to simplify testing with functional test systems. The 1796 software system, called CAPS X, contains a library of over 2000 SSI and MSI devices and 100 LSI devices from which it draws during program preparation.

Hewlett-Packard 3062A Board Test System

The HP3062A combines in-circuit and functional test capabilities and can test digital, analog, and hybrid circuits. The combining of the ICT and functional test capabilities is a popular trend and arises from the demand for both types of testers. Users often run in-circuit tests first to locate basic faults in the boards. They then run functional tests to increase yields at the next levels of testing and product assembly. By combining both capabilities in one ATE system, the overall cost is lowered.

The HP3062A has a built-in HP-IB (IEEE-488) bus capability. It uses a series 200 computer as a controller. In its ICT mode, the HP3062A performs in-circuit and short circuit tests. In its functional test and fault diagnosis mode, it applies signals to the board and makes measurements at output nodes.

The HP3062A has an extensive software system. The controller uses HPL (Hewlett-Packard's language) as its operating language. The HP3062A's Board Test Language (BTL) is the high-level language used to program board tests. The HP3062A has an in-circuit program generator (IPG) software system that creates the board test programs and the specifications for wiring the test fixture for the board to be tested. The user must enter the device type, value, tolerance, and location of the interconnection nodes into the IPG. A CAD (computer-aided design) system data base or other offline system can economically provide this data. The IPG creates a short circuit–open circuit test procedure and contains a procedure for automatically learning the short circuit characteristics of the board. A data logging package also gathers and analyzes test data whenever a UUT fails. Software developed for the HP3060A, the predecessor of the HP3062A, is compatible with the 3062A.

The HP3062A tests microprocessor circuits, ROMs, RAMs, and I/O-based circuit boards at their operating speeds through the use of signature analysis. It provides stimulus at up to a 2-MHz rate and measurements at up to 10 MHz.

Zehntel 900

The 900 is an in-circuit tester that handles large, complex boards, including those with mixed logic, such as ECL (emitter-coupled logic), TTL (transis-

Fig. 1-9   Hewlett-Packard 3062A Board Test System *(right fore-ground)*, the Series 200 computer *(left)*, and the HP3061A Board Test System *(background)*. *(Courtesy of Hewlett-Packard Company.)*

tor-transistor logic), and CMOS (complementary metal-oxide semiconductor). The 900 is shown in Fig. 1-10.

The fixture for the 900 contains 3024 universal test points through which it tests digital and analog components and measures resistances. It performs its resistance measurements at 200 mV to avoid biasing semiconductor junctions.

Each node of the fixture connects to its own driver/sensor circuitry. To do this, the 900 uses 63 driver/receiver cards. Each card contains 12 microcircuits, and each microcircuit contains circuitry for four test nodes ($4 \times 12 \times 63 = 3024$ test nodes). The software controls each node simultaneously. Since the power supplies of each driver/ receiver card are programmable from -6 to $+12$ V, one can program each card separately for any logic family within the range.

The 900 isolates each device and performs the tests contained in its Data Director Library. The Library contains such LSI/VLSI devices as the 8080,

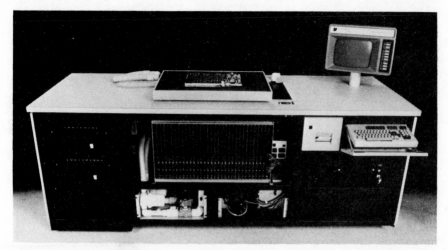

Fig. 1-10 Zehntel 900 in-circuit test system. Notice the vacuum hose connected to the test fixture. The open front on the system reveals the driver-receiver cards below the test fixture. *(Courtesy of Zehntel.)*

6800, Z80, Z8008, and 16-bit microprocessors. The 900 runs at 2 MHz, a fairly high rate for ICTs, and uses signature analysis to handle the large amount of digital data. It compares bit-stream signatures at each test node with an expected value to determine if the node is faulty.

Fairchild 3500 In-Circuit Test System

The 3500 takes an economical approach to the testing of circuit boards. The operator connects a test clip to each device on the board in turn and the 3500 tests that device. The operator then moves the test clip to the next device and repeats the process. This method reduces the number of pin electronics required and eliminates the need for a test fixture. This makes it practical for low-volume testing. The 3500 is shown in Fig. 1-11. A block diagram is shown in Fig. 1-12.

The 3500 tests TTL, ECL, CMOS, RTL (resistor-transistor logic), and DTL (diode-transistor logic) systems. Each pin has a 1024 × 4 bit RAM for high-speed parallel test pattern bursts. It can test ICs up to 40 pins, but its capability is expandable in 4-pin increments up to 128 pins, so it can handle LSI, as well as MSI and SSI, devices. The system can also be used for functional testing.

The 3500 uses the Data General Nova 4C computer as a controller. The Nova 4C utilizes a 12.5 megabyte Winchester disk and a 1.25 megabyte floppy disk. A strip printer provides failure reports that the operator can attach to the defective board as a repair message.

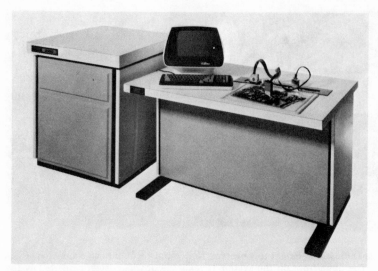

Fig. 1-11 Fairchild 3500 In-Circuit Test System. A test probe is connected to a board on the work surface. *(Courtesy of Fairchild Subassembly Test Systems. Titusville, Fla.)*

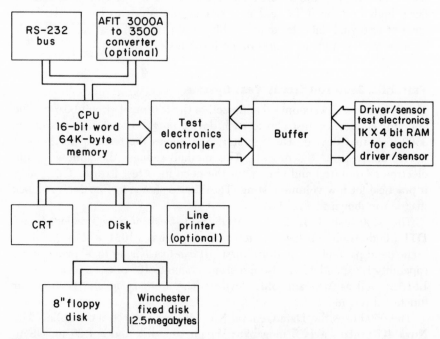

Fig. 1-12 Block Diagram of the 3500. Note the 1K × 4 bit RAM for each driver/sensor. *(Courtesy of Fairchild Subassembly Test System, Titusville, Fla.)*

The 3500 contains a device library on the disk. To develop a board test, the programmer enters a list of the devices on the board and the identifier for each one in the order to be tested. The 3500 transfers the tests for those devices from the library to the data file for the board. The programmer may specify the order in which the 3500 executes the tests, or the software can control it automatically. The programmer can also make changes as required in the individual programs.

Teradyne L200 Board Test System

The L200 performs both functional and in-circuit testing of analog and digital circuit boards from 10 MHz down to static tests. It uses a DEC PDP 11/44 computer as a controller. The PDP 11/44 uses the Unibus for internal bus activities. It contains up to 4 megabytes of main memory, up to four 10-megabyte cartridge disks, and dual floppy disks.

The test station portion contains a Digital Command Processor, a high-speed microprogrammable DMA (direct memory access) processor that transfers patterns from the controller memory to channel cards. The channel cards determine the basic capability of the L200. A user can combine up to 48 digital and 48 analog channel cards, as shown in Table 1-1, to achieve the level of testing desired. The dynamic test patterns are transferred from local channel memory to the board under test. The responses are compared with the expected response stored in memory to make a pass-fail decision.

Fig. 1-13   Teradyne L200 Board Test System. The probe for locating faults lies across the top of the fixture. *(Courtesy of Teradyne, Inc.)*

Table 1-1

Channel card	Capability	Speed	Channels/card
DI	Digital functional and in-circuit	10 MHz	8
DII	Digital functional and in-circuit	5 MHz	8
DIII	Digital functional and in-circuit	5 MHz	24
AI	Analog functional and in-circuit	5 MHz	24

The user can configure the L200 for vacuum bed-of-nails or edge connector interfacing to the UUT. The fixture is designed to keep the lead length from the channel card to the board under test to 10 cm (4 in) or less. The significance of this feature will become apparent in the discussion of hardware reliability in a later chapter.

An analog instrumentation group at the rear racks of the L200 contains analog stimuli, measuring devices, and programmable power supplies. This group provides analog in-circuit and functional testing of analog and hybrid circuit boards. The group includes a DMM, a dc measurement system, voltage and current sources, a function generator, and a timer-counter.

An option is available to test board memories. The Algorithmic Pattern Processor (APP) has a microprogrammable address generation capability of 24 bits and a data generation capability of up to 72 bits. The APP provides such standard memory test algorithms as GALPAT, MARCH, and WALK, as well as user-microprogrammed algorithms.

The L200 contains a number of software packages. Its In-Circuit Composer automatically generates an in-circuit test program from a physical description of the board for both analog and digital components. It elects the required stimuli, measurements, and guarding for testing of resistance, capacitance, inductance, semiconductor junctions, and transistor gain. The well-known LASAR software package facilitates the generation of programs for the functional test of complex digital LSI boards as well as component patterns for in-circuit testing.

The user can also generate a program manually with the interactive text editor of the L200, which checks input errors automatically, then compiles the test program. The L200 also contains a debugging software package that allows the programmer to alter the program flow interactively, interrogate and modify system hardware, and execute immediate commands. Within seconds, permanent changes to the source level program can be edited and compiled, linked, and then executed.

The L200 also contains a number of diagnostic packages. INCITER (In-Circuit Test Evaluator) analyzes test failures and diagnoses short and open circuits and component failures. The State Sensitive Trace (SST) package handles failures that occur during digital functional testing. When the L200 has edge-connector fixturing, SST provides guided-probe instructions to a nontechnical operator. When it uses bed-of-nails fixturing, it probes the test nodes automatically through the fixture pins. A later chapter will discuss the L200 diagnostics.

Julie Research Locost 106

The LOCOST 106 represents a twist in ATE, the use of automatic techniques to perform calibration of test equipment. The LOCOST 106 is in effect an automated calibration laboratory. It contains fundamental standards and sources that allow automated test and calibration of such test equipment as meters (ac and dc, digital and panel), high-current shunts, and oscilloscopes, among others. The LOCOST 106 is shown in Fig. 1-14.

EML Automation PCB Handler

Fig. 1-15 shows a useful device for the printed circuit board production line. EML Automation's PCB Handler provides automated handling, loading, and testing of boards. The user can configure the handler for testing of either bare boards or assembled boards. An operator is required occasionally

Fig. 1-14 Julie LOCOST 106 for automated calibration of test equipment. *(Courtesy of Julie Research Labs, Inc.)*

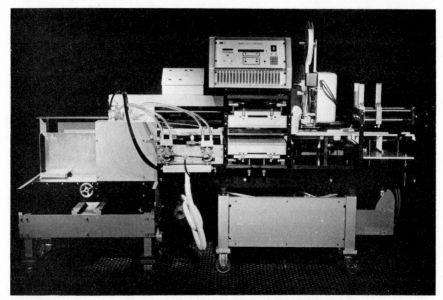

Fig. 1-15 EML Automation PCB Handler. The boards are stacked at the left. The handler picks them up and feeds them through one at a time. The tester mounted at the top center performs the required tests. The completed boards are then fed toward the right. *(Courtesy of EML Automation, Inc.)*

to stack a new batch of boards (unless the handler is fed by conveyor) on the infeed module and remove the tested boards from the outfeed module. The handler lifts the boards, transfers them to the test section, runs the tests, then transfers the boards to the output stack. The bed-of-nails fixture can be actuated pneumatically or by means of a vacuum.

The handler contains no testing capability of its own. It must be fitted with a short circuit–continuity tester, shown with the handler in the illustration. The handler will process most rectangular boards up to 686 mm (27 in) × 686 mm at a production rate of up to 60 boards per minute.

The user selects the feed modules for the handler that fit the particular production needs. The following are the variations available.

1. Stack infeed/outfeed modules are used for bare printed circuit boards. The infeed operates continuously as long as boards are available. It lifts each board and places it on the conveyor slides, where it is transferred to the test fixture. The outfeeds can be used to sort accepted, open circuit, and short circuit boards.

2. Conveyor infeed/outfeed modules interface with existing conveyors.

3. Rack infeed/outfeed handles loaded printed circuit boards. The racks can be used for transportation and storage.

Each module may be used in combination with others to suit the production line requirements. The handler can be configured with rack in, conveyor out; conveyor in, stack out, etc. The PCB Handler can integrate with a production line and can be configured to insert components and apply serial numbers and bar codes.

IN-HOUSE ATE SYSTEMS

A number of organizations build ATE systems in-house and use them to test their own products. This practice can evolve to the point where the organization develops a standard product line. The organization's software group generally provides the necessary test and self-test programs, as well as any diagnostic routines. Organizations that build ATE systems in-house can tailor them to the specific needs of the UUTs that they must test.

Fig. 1-16 shows an Antenna Electronics Test Set built for in-house use by Westinghouse Electric Corporation. A block diagram is shown in Fig.

Fig. 1-16 Example of an ATE system designed and built for in-house use. The operator interfaces through the keyboard and touch-sensitive CRT. The UUT mounts on a fixture that provides a mechanical and electrical interface and directs the cooling air over the UUT. *(Courtesy of Westinghouse Electric Corp.)*

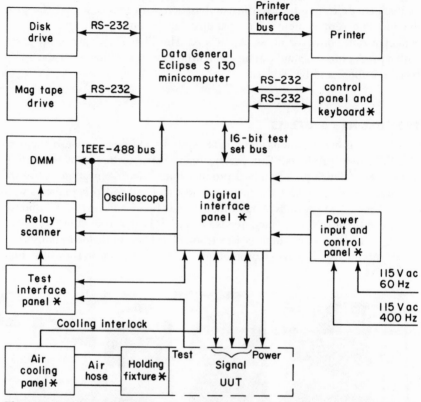

Fig. 1-17 Block diagram of the in-house ATE system in Fig. 1-16. An asterisk indicates items built in-house. *(Courtesy of Westinghouse Electric Corp.)*

1-17. Westinghouse uses the system to test the antenna electronics assembly of one of its fire control radars. The test set uses a Data General Eclipse S-130 minicomputer with a disk drive as a controller. A magnetic tape unit allows the programmer to prepare revisions in the software laboratory and to enter them on the disk when they are completed.

The panels that were built in-house include the following:

1. The power input and control panel, which contains the main circuit breakers and relays necessary to provide operating power to the test set.

2. The interface panel, which connects UUT test signals to the relay scanner switching system.

3. The air cooling panel, which provides cooling air to the UUT. An air pressure switch in the air stream senses when the airflow is adequate and enables the UUT input power. This interlock prevents damage to the UUT that would result from an inadequate flow of cooling air.

4. The control panel and keyboard, which features a touch-sensitive CRT that allows the operator to select various tests and other parameters without a lengthy keyboard entry. The keyboard allows entry of such information as serial number, date, and model number. It also allows the programmer to load, store, and change programs.

5. The digital interface panel, which contains the circuitry necessary for testing the UUT. It is the main control panel for the test set and contains UUT power switches, status lights, and test circuits.

6. The holding fixture, which provides a mechanical base to hold the UUT and provide a path for the flow of air over the UUT. A cable provides the electrical connection between the UUT test connector and the digital interface panel.

The test set contains a DMM for voltage measurements and a relay scanner to connect the various test points to the DMM. The controller interfaces with other items in the test set over an RS-232C bus and a dedicated 16-bit test set bus.

SUMMARY

ATE has many advantages over manual methods. ATE runs tests faster, is more consistent, experiences fewer errors, and costs less per test. A less skilled operator can perform routine tests and free skilled technicians for a level of work more suited to their capabilities.

The use of ATE will never eliminate the technician, however. Technicians must still perform the alignment and troubleshooting. (The ATE system can assist here with diagnostic software.) Technicians are now more productive with ATE than they were with test benches and manual test sets.

The disadvantages of ATE are few, but significant. They cost more than manual test sets on the average (but they often pay for themselves in a few years if they are utilized properly). Reliability can sometimes also be a problem: Because of the complex mix of hardware and software, it is difficult to assure that the ATE cycles through the tests exactly as it should. Since the advantages of ATE outweigh the disadvantages, however, the need for ATE will rise rapidly in the future.

REFERENCES

Carlson, A. W.: "Self-Designed Test Systems Can Make Good Design Sense," *EDN*, Sept. 2, 1981, pp. 235–240.

Carrol, Michael P., and Gerald W. Petersen: "In-Circuit Tester Takes On ECL, TTL, and MOS Devices," *Electronic Design*, May 28, 1981, pp. 91–97.

Hopkins, Robert L.: "Meeting the Challenge of Automated ECL Testing," *Computer Design*, Sept. 1980, pp. 115–122.

Jessen, Ken: "In-Circuit Tester Answers μP-board Challenge," *Electronic Design*, Nov. 8, 1980, pp. 97–101.

Liguori, F.: *Automated Test Equipment: Hardware, Software, and Management*, IEEE Press, New York, 1974, pp. 29–105.

Martel, Robert: "A Users Approach to an ATE Multi-Option Tester," *ATE Seminar/Exhibit Preview Guide, Electronics Test*, May 1982, pp. 52–59.

McLeod, Jonah: "ATE Swings toward Merged In-Circuit, Functional Tests," *Electronic Design*, Oct. 29, 1981, pp. 90–104.

Nagy, Alex, Allan Futterman, and Hoshang Vaid: "Automatic Calibration Sharpens VLSI Testing," *Electronic Design*, Apr. 29, 1981, pp. 205–210.

Raymond, Douglas W.: "In-Circuit Testing Comes of Age," *Computer Design*, Aug. 1981, pp. 117–124.

Runyon, Stan: "Testing LSI-Based Boards: Many Issues, Many Answers," *Electronic Design*, Mar. 15, 1979, pp. 58–66.

Runyon, Stanley: "ATE Revolution Erupts, with Software a Key Inciter," *Electronic Design*, Oct. 28, 1982, pp. 102–114.

Teague, Dane: "Automatic Power Supply Testing," *Electronic Products*, Apr. 1981, pp. 63–65.

Weisberg, Martin J.: "Production-Phase Testing Increases Product Throughput," *EDN*, Mar. 20, 1980, pp. 195–202.

2

THE GPIB:
AN INTRODUCTION

The advantages of a standardized interface bus were realized many years before the GPIB became reality. Each manufacturer used its own method of interfacing, and the chaos that practice engendered threatened the future possibilities of ATE. Hewlett-Packard began work on a standardized bus in 1965 and eventually developed its HP-IB, or Hewlett-Packard Interface Bus. In 1975, IEEE published its *IEEE-488-1975 Digital Interface for Programmable Instrumentation,* which set up the GPIB essentially as it exists today. In 1978, IEEE issued IEEE-488-1978, an expanded version of the 1975 standard.

Soon after the publication of the IEEE standard, other organizations completed their research and published their GPIB standards. The American National Standards Institute (ANSI) published its *MC1.1 Digital Interface for Programmable Instrumentation* and the International Electrotechnical Commission (IEC) issued its *IEC 625-1 An Interface System for Programmable Measuring Apparatus (Byte Serial Bit Parallel).* Both standards essentially conform to the IEEE standard. IEC 625-1 differs from the IEEE/ANSI version only in the type of interface connector specified.

THE GPIB: AN OVERVIEW

The standards set the mechanical, electrical, and functional specifications for the interface. With this information, design engineers can design a device with an interface that is mechanically, electrically, and functionally compatible with other devices on the bus.

Each device connects to the bus by means of the IEEE-488 (or IEC-625-1) cable, which terminates at each end with a stackable 24-pin connector. The IEEE-488 cable is shown in Fig. 2-1. The IEEE-488/ANSI connectors

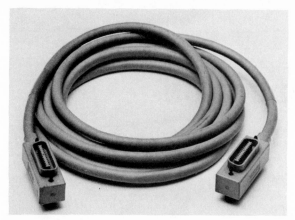

Fig. 2-1 IEEE-488 interconnection cable. The cables are designed to be stacked. The user connects one end of the cable to the instrument and the other end to any other such connector in the system connected to the bus. *(Courtesy of Racal-Dana Instruments Inc.)*

differ from the IEC-625-1 cable, as shown in Fig. 2-2a and Fig. 2-2b. The mechanical connection to the bus therefore requires only that one plug a cable into the device's IEEE-488 connector and then plug the other end into the cable connector of another device already on this bus.

One may connect up to 15 devices on a bus, which generally means 14 devices and a controller. The total cable length can run 20 meters overall or 2 meters per device, whichever is less. One may connect the devices in a star or linear pattern, or a combination of the two.

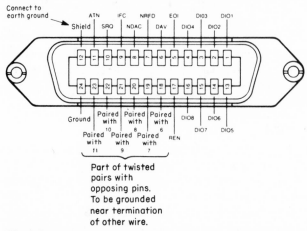

Fig. 2-2a Pin arrangement for the IEEE-488 connector. (*Courtesy of Hewlett-Packard Company.*)

(Horizontal)

Contact	Signal line	Contact	Signal line
1	DIO1	14	DIO 5
2	DIO 2	15	DIO 6
3	DIO 3	16	DIO 7
4	DIO 4	17	DIO 8
5	REN	18	Gnd (5)
6	EOI	19	Gnd (6)
7	DAV	20	Gnd (7)
8	NRFD	21	Gnd (8)
9	NDAC	22	Gnd (9)
10	IFC	23	Gnd (10)
11	SRQ	24	Gnd (11)
12	ATN	25	Gnd (12)
13	Shield		

Fig. 2-2b Pin arrangement for the IEC-625-1 connector. *(Courtesy of Hewlett-Packard Company.)*

The standards do omit the operational characteristics of the bus devices, however, and leave message format to the discretion of the designer. As a result, a controller message that sets a DMM to ac volts will vary with the particular requirements of the DMM as set by the manufacturer. The message format for a Racal-Dana 6000, for example, differs from a Systron-Donner 7344A. A later chapter will go into message formats in more detail.

LISTENERS, TALKERS, AND CONTROLLERS

The GPIB uses a party-line architecture, in that all devices connect in parallel and share the signal lines. This architecture is illustrated in Fig. 2-3. Each device on the bus can *listen*, *talk*, or *control*, or perform combinations of the three functions. The following is a description of each type of device.

Listener

These devices accept data and commands from the bus, generally when the controller addresses them as listeners. Examples of devices that can only listen are displays, printers, and power supplies. Such devices receive commands, but they never make measurements and therefore never have to send data over the bus.

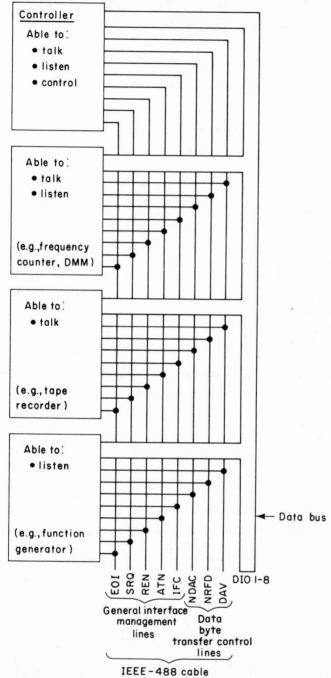

Fig. 2-3 The IEEE-488 architecture consists of three groups of lines, the data bus, data byte transfer control lines, and the general interface management lines. Note that devices vary in their capabilities to talk, listen, and control.

Talker

These devices send data over the bus to the active listeners, generally when a controller addresses them as a talker. Only one talker may be active on the bus at a time. An example of a device that can only talk is a tape recorder. Many devices in a GPIB system, however, have a dual capability and can both talk and listen. Devices that make measurements, such as a counter or DMM, must talk to send the measurement data over the bus. The DMM and counter are also listeners in that they must receive data from the bus in order to set them up.

Controller

This device was discussed in Chap. 1. The controller manages the bus, sends commands, receives data and status, and controls the flow of data. As a result, the system controller acts as a talker (to send commands and data) and as a listener (to receive data and status). Only one controller can have command of the bus at a time. It can pass control to another controller on the bus, however, and assume a talker-listener role.

ADDRESSING

In order to command particular devices to do something, the controller must first send the address of the device. Each device has its own unique address, which the user can set by switches or jumpers on the device itself. The factory usually sets the address to a particular value, but most devices are capable of being changed. A number of devices have address switches on the rear panel, as shown in Fig. 2-4.

The addresses can range from 0 to 31, although address 31 is generally unused because it serves as an "unlisten" or "untalk" command to disable active listeners or the talker on a bus.

The following illustrates a format for addressing:

	Bit number						
	6	5	4	3	2	1	0
Bus command	0	0	C	C	C	C	C
Listen address:	0	1	L	L	L	L	L
Talk address:	1	0	T	T	T	T	T
Secondary address:	1	1	S	S	S	S	S

C, L, T, and S represent bits in the respective addresses. Of the seven bits of the data line (an eighth bit is generally unused here), the lowest five (bits 0 through 4) set the address. Bits 5 and 6 determine the class of information, which can be a talk or listen address, commands, or secondary addresses.

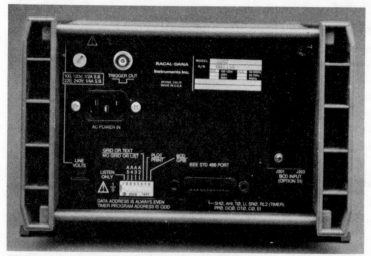

Fig. 2-4 Rear panel of an instrument with IEEE-488 capability. Note the address switches to the left of center at the bottom and the IEEE-488 connector to the right. *(Courtesy of Racal-Dana Instruments Inc.)*

Some devices use two addresses. The primary address controls the device itself. The secondary address may control a function within the device. In a plotter, for example, the primary address will set up the plotter interface. The secondary address may lift or lower the pen.

Once the user sets the address to a particular value, no other device on the bus can use that address. If the ATE system has a multiple-bus architecture and the controller manages more than one bus, the user may set the same address on an alternate bus, but must avoid duplicate addresses on the same bus. Once the operator has set the addresses, the controller can individually address each device on the bus.

DETAILS OF THE GPIB

As illustrated in Fig. 2-3, the GPIB consists of three separate groups of lines: the *data bus, data byte transfer control lines,* and *general interface management lines.* These 16 lines, along with 8 return lines, make up the GPIB. The explanation below covers HP-IB and IEEE-488.

Data Bus

These eight signal lines handle addresses, commands, measurement data, and status. Commands from the controller and measurement data from the

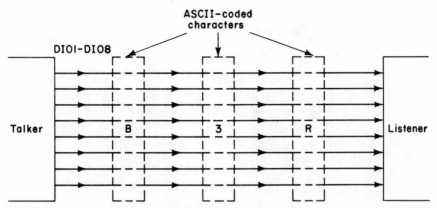

Fig. 2-5 Data travels in a bit parallel—byte serial format. In this case, the string "R3B" is sent over the data bus.

test equipment, for example, pass over this bus. Data travels in a bit parallel–byte serial format, as illustrated in Fig. 2-5. The data conforms to the ASCII (American Standard for Information Interchange) code, although other codes can be used for such reasons as data compression and speed. The international equivalent of the ASCII code is the ISO (International Standards Organization) code.

Data Byte Transfer Control

These three lines control the byte transfer of data. Some texts call the group the handshake bus because data transfer takes place only when all instruments involved indicate they are ready for transfer. Fig. 2-6 illustrates the timing sequence of these lines. The three lines and their functions in the control of data transfer are described below.

NRFD (Not Ready for Data) The active listeners (those the controller has addressed to listen) control the status of this line. Until all active listeners are ready to accept data from the source, they keep their NRFD line at a logic low. Since all devices interface in parallel with the bus, even one listener unready to accept data will keep the line low.

As each listener becomes ready for data transfer, it sets its NRFD line high. NRFD operates in an interlocked handshake mode, which requires that all active listeners be ready to accept data before the line itself changes to a logic high. NRFD therefore operates at the speed of the slowest acceptor to respond. Only when the last listener sets its NRFD line to a high does the line follow and rise to a high. A high NRFD signal indicates to the talker that all devices are now ready to receive data.

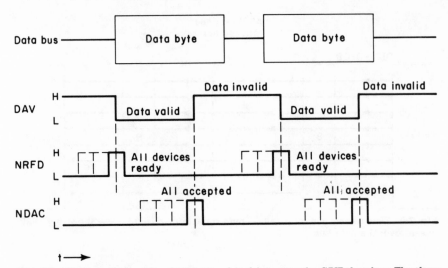

Fig. 2-6 Timing relationships during transfer of data over the GPIB data bus. The three lines involved are sometimes called the handshake bus because data transfer takes place only when all devices have signaled that they are ready for the transfer.

DAV (Data Valid) This line indicates the validity of the data on the data bus. The active data source, the talker, controls the status of this line. Until its data is valid, the talker keeps DAV high. When the data becomes valid, the talker sets DAV to a low, which signals the active listeners on the bus that the data is valid and they can now accept it.

One may understand the status of the lines better if it is realized that the bus operates in a low-true configuration. A logic low thus indicates true, which may be opposite to what one might expect. When NRFD is a low, it is true, which means that the devices are *not* ready for data. The same reasoning may be used for the opposite case when NRFD is a logic high. When DAV is set low, it is true and the data is valid.

NDAC (Not Data Accepted) The active listeners also control this line. After the talker sets DAV low, the active listeners read in the data from the bus. Each listener keeps NDAC low while it reads in the data. As each one completes the data transfer, it sets its NDAC line to a high. As with NRFD, however, the NDAC line stays low until *all* active listeners have accepted the data. At that time, NDAC goes to a high. The data transfer is complete and bus control returns to the controller.

General Interface Management Lines

These lines perform control and status functions on the bus. Unlike multiline commands, which will be discussed later, each line here is dedicated to a specific function. A signal on one of these lines will result in a unique action. A description of each of these five dedicated lines follows:

ATN (Attention) This line indicates the nature of the data on the data bus. There are two possible modes: commands and data.

1. If ATN is low, the controller has placed a command on the bus. All listeners and talkers must accept the command and act on it as ordered. In this mode, the controller also addresses devices to be active listeners or talkers.

2. If ATN is high, the information on the bus is data and all *active* listeners (as designated when ATN was low) must accept the data from the active talker. Any other devices on the bus remain in the "idle" state during this time.

IFC (Interface Clear) This line sets the bus to an idle state. The controller "unaddresses" talker and listeners and halts all operations. This action generally occurs when something goes wrong on the bus.

REN (Remote Enable) This line controls the remote-local status of the devices on the line with this capability. When REN goes true, the affected device switches to remote operation and comes under control of the bus. When REN goes false, the device switches to local operation and an operator can control it locally, usually from the front panel.

SRQ (Service Request) Any device with SRQ capability can use the SRQ line as an interrupt. A device utilizes the SRQ line to alert the controller that it requires attention, such as when it has measurement data ready for transmission to the controller. When the controller is free, it can service the request.

ATE systems can use this line in a number of ways. An instrument with computational capability can make a number of measurements and perform computations (average, peak reading, etc.) on the values without tying up the controller. When the instrument has completed the measurements and calculations, it can alert the controller with the SRQ line and pass on the results of the computations.

EOI (End Or Identify) This line operates with the ATN line to perform two major functions. The controller sets both ATN and EOI true to initiate a *parallel poll* operation. A parallel poll allows the controller to obtain information from a device with parallel poll capability. Each device returns a status bit on one of the data lines. The particular data line can be set with switches or jumpers or by the controller. When ATN is false, EOI indicates the latest byte in a data message.

The data byte transfer control and general interface management groups operate on dedicated lines in the bus architecture. A number of *multiline* commands of the GPIB standards utilize the data lines instead. These are universal commands, addressed commands, and secondary commands.

UNIVERSAL COMMANDS

The GPIB utilizes universal commands that affect every device configured to respond to that command. The four lines of the general interface management group (IFC, ATN, REN, EOI) comprise the uniline universal commands. Optional multiline commands are also available. They are described as follows:

1. *DCL (Device Clear):* This command resets all devices with DCL capability, whether the controller has addressed them or not. The reset state will vary with each device and is generally described in the manufacturer's manual.

2. *LLO (Local Lockout):* This command disables the capability to return to local. It would thus disable a front panel Local switch. To restore the local capability after this command, the controller must set REN false.

3. *SPE (Serial Poll Enable):* This command is similar to the parallel poll, except that the controller polls each device in turn. The polled device responds with a status byte when the controller addresses it to talk. One of the purposes of a poll is to determine which device sent a service request.

4. *SPD (Serial Poll Disable):* This command disables the serial poll operation and returns the devices involved to a normal talker state.

5. *PPU (Parallel Poll Unconfigure):* This command resets devices with parallel poll capability to the idle state.

ADDRESSED AND SECONDARY COMMANDS

As with other commands, addressed commands affect only those devices with the capability to respond. The controller must generally address a device as a listener before it can respond to an addressed command. Secondary commands are used in conjunction with other commands or an address. The following is a description of these commands:

1. *GET (Group Execute Trigger):* This command triggers all applicable devices and causes them to initiate preprogrammed actions simultaneously.

ATE can use this command to trigger a sequence of stimuli and measurement actions.

2. *GTL (Go to Local):* This command causes the addressed device to initiate its local control. It leaves the remote state and the operator gains front panel control.

3. *SDC (Selected Device Clear):* This command resets the addressed device to a particular state. As with the DCL command described above, the particular state will vary with each device.

4. *TCT (Take Control):* This command allows the present controller to pass control of the bus to another controller on the bus.

5. *PPC (Parallel Poll Configure):* This command causes the addressed listener to respond to the secondary commands Parallel Poll Enable (PPE) and Parallel Poll Disable (PPD), which follow the PPC command. PPE commands a device with parallel poll capability to respond on a particular data line. PPD disables the device from responding to the parallel poll.

SUBSET CAPABILITIES

IEEE-488 provides enormous flexibility to the design engineer. It provides a number of *subset* capabilities from which designers may select as many as they wish in order to give a device the desired GPIB capability. A list of subset capabilities available under IEEE-488 is given in Appendix A. The standard recommends that manufactures mark a device's subset capabilities near the bus connector, as shown in Fig. 2-4 and 2-7.

IEEE STD 488 PORT

Fig. 2-7 Preferred method of marking subset capabilities at the IEEE-488 port on an instrument. *(Courtesy of Hewlett-Packard Company.)*

SH1, AH1, T2, L1, SR1, RL2, PP2, DC1, DT0, C0, E1

SUMMARY

The IEEE/ANSI/IEC standard GPIB allows one to interface instruments together in an ATE system. The standard defines functional, electrical, and mechanical aspects of the bus, but avoids the operational aspects. A number of commands are available to facilitate bus control. The standard includes a number of optional subset capabilities that a designer may include in the design of a device to give it the desired GPIB capability.

REFERENCES

Anudson, Robert L.: "2nd-Generation GPIB Equipment Offers Easy-to-Use Improvements," *EDN*, Aug. 19, 1981, pp. 165–172.

IEEE Standard Digital Interface for Programmable Instrumentation, ANSI/IEEE STD 488-1978 with Supplement IEEE STD 488A-1980, Institute of Electrical and Electronic Engineers, Inc., July 25, 1980.

Laengrich, Norbert: "Instrument Intelligence Determines 488 Bus Speed," *Electronic Design*, Oct. 15, 1981, pp. 181–185.

Leibson, Steve: "The Standard Interface—HP-IB," *Keyboard*, July–Aug. 1981, pp. 8–11.

Rony, Peter D.: "Interfacing Fundamentals: Bused Flags," *Computer Design*, July 1981, pp. 162–168.

Tilden, Mark and Bob Ramirez: "GPIB Software Configuration Determines System Performance," *EDN*, Aug. 4, 1982, pp. 137–142.

———— and ————: "Understanding IEEE-488 Basics Simplifies System Integration," *EDN*, June 9, 1982, pp. 121–129.

Tutorial Description of the Hewlett-Packard Interface Bus, Hewlett-Packard Co., Nov. 1980, pp. 2–50.

Wiseman, Carmen D.: "IEEE-488—The General Purpose Interface Bus," *Electronics Test*, Apr. 1981, pp. 52–63.

Yates, Warren: "Getting aboard the GPIB," *Electronic Products*, Feb. 1979, pp. 43–48.

3

ATE BUILDING BLOCKS

Chap. 1 covered the basic elements of ATE, including the controller, stimuli, measuring instruments, switching system, and test fixture. The controller will be discussed in a later chapter. This chapter will cover the other elements of ATE systems.

A basic requirement for ATE is that the controller must have some method of communicating with the various parts of the ATE system. This communication usually occurs over the IEEE-488 bus or another such bus, such as the RS-232C serial or GPIO (general purpose input-output) parallel buses. If the device manufacturer fails to include the capability of bus control, the operator would have to control that device manually. This could reduce the ATE test speed to that of a semiautomated or manual test set.

The ATE should also optimize its automation of the test as much as possible. The use of built-in "intelligence" in instruments may provide extra capability or speed. Only through automation can the user realize the economic advantages of ATE. On the other hand, one should be careful to avoid specifying unnecessary capabilities. The addition of intelligent instruments would be wasteful, for example, if the ATE system never uses such a capability.

"INTELLIGENT" INSTRUMENTS

Since the 1970s, test equipment manufacturers have produced so-called intelligent (or smart) instruments with internal program and data storage and computing capability. Soft keys have replaced front panel controls to allow the operator to input control instructions to the instrument's microprocessor logic. Some instruments allow the operator or controller to store a number of instrument setups, then call them up later with a simple command.

Instrument intelligence has a number of advantages. For one, it can reduce the traffic on the bus if the programmer uses the intelligence properly. The instrument can perform calculations and make measurements in order to reduce a sequence of measurements to a single value. During this time, the controller can perform other tasks. When it can break free after receiving an SRQ message from the instrument, it reads in the result. An instrument without this capability would have to send the entire collection of measurements one by one over the bus. Intelligence can thus reduce the overall test time.

Uses of "Smart" Instruments

Let us suppose that a particular test requires the controller to compute the average of 150 voltage readings. An intelligent DMM could handle the data gathering and computation tasks while the controller does other things. The entire test program could be read into the DMM at the start of the test and the controller can call it up through the use of a single bus message. After the DMM has completed the measurements, it computes the average and stores it. The controller will read in the result whenever it can and use that average value as it would if it had computed the result itself.

Fig. 3-1 shows an example of the use of an intelligent ac voltmeter. The UUTs reside in a temperature chamber during a burn-in test. The test

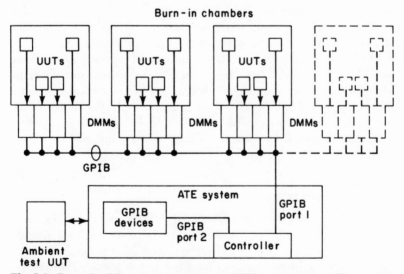

Fig. 3-1 Example of the use of an intelligent DMM to relieve the ATE controller of some tasks. The DMMs take readings every 15 s at UUT test points, make computations, then inform the controller when the results are ready for transfer over the data bus.

requires that the voltmeters take a reading every 15 s, then compute the average and find the maximum and minimum readings.

If the ATE system uses an intelligent voltmeter, the controller can be utilized for other tests during the burn-in period. The voltmeters take a reading every 15 s, as the controller programmed them to do. At the end of the test, they determine the final values of average, maximum, and minimum readings. When the controller finishes its tasks, it can read in the values. The controller can thus control a number of burn-in chambers and test other types of UUTs under ambient test at the same time. It can even be used elsewhere during the burn-in test. This illustration is given for explanatory purposes; other methods are available to accomplish the same purpose.

Drawbacks of Intelligent Instruments

Intelligent instruments do have some drawbacks. Their cost often runs higher than conventional instruments, for example, and the tests for particular UUTs may be unable to utilize the capabilities. If a test never requires computation of peak reading, for example, the system would gain nothing if the ATE design engineer included a DMM with that capability.

Although intelligent instruments can reduce the time for tests, such a reduction could be meaningless if the ATE system used the function so seldom that its effect on test time was insignificant. If the averaging capability is used twice in an hour, for example, and saves 6 s each time, the capability would be wasted. If the routine were used every few seconds, on the other hand, the savings in test time could be considerable.

The ability of the "intelligent" device to save test program memory can also mislead the ATE designer, since the controller could require as much or more memory to set up a special function than it would to perform the task itself. Unless the instrument has its programs built in or allows program entry from the controller over the bus or through a storage medium (e.g., cassette, floppy disk), the operator must enter the program each time the instrument is turned on or another program is read over it. The latter occurs often in ATE systems that test a number of different types of UUTs each day.

The potential user of intelligent instruments must thus evaluate all aspects of need and use beforehand. Properly utilized, an intelligent instrument could relieve the controller and the bus of many time-consuming functions. Test equipment manufacturers frequently point out that they make each generation of their instruments "smarter." As instruments gain capabilities that will allow controllers to down-load many of the functions they would ordinarily perform, the intelligent instrument will become more and more cost-effective for use in ATE.

DRIVER/SENSOR

Most in-circuit test systems for digital devices use driver/sensors at the pins of the test fixtures. The driver provides the stimuli to the pin while the sensor reads in the signal at the pin and passes it on to the test system.

Fig. 3-2 illustrates typical driver/sensor pin electronics. The controller can program the driver and sensor in this system for two different logic families within the available voltage levels to match the logic families of the circuit under test at that pin. The ICT can thus test boards with mixed logic families. (Note that sensors are also commonly called "receivers.")

The controller generally sends the test pattern data to the driver for output to the circuit or commands sensors to read in the signal at that pin. During dynamic testing, the test pattern rate may become quite high and exceed the overall capability of the controller. A RAM connected at the pin provides memory to store patterns and responses in order to run the test

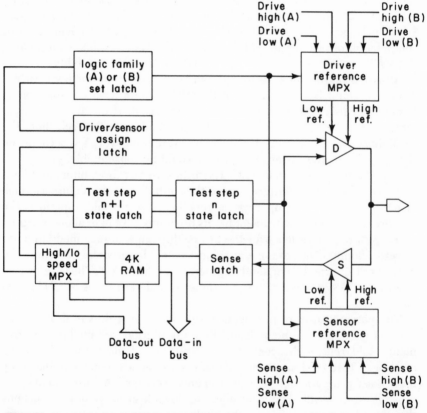

Fig. 3-2 Block diagram of typical driver/sensor pin electronics. Note the connection of the driver (D) and sensor (S) to the pin. Each pin in this system has 4K of RAM and can be programmed for dual-logic families. (*Courtesy of GenRad, Inc., Concord, Mass.*)

at a faster rate. In many cases, this method allows the ATE system to test the UUT at its operating speed.

STIMULI

ATE stimuli provide the signals for the testing of the UUT. Such signals can take many forms, including a TTL logic level, a complex waveform, and a pulsed RF (radio frequency) signal. The following are examples of stimuli found in ATE:

1. Power supplies

2. Generators (audio, RF, function, pulse)

3. Digital to analog converters

4. Pin drivers (discussed above)

Function Generators

A function generator represents a moderate amount of complexity for bus operation. Once the user has hooked up the GPIB cable between the bus and the function generator, the problem arises of getting the correct output signals from the function generator.

At this point, of course, its operation becomes more a problem of software than of hardware. The program must set up the function generator to deliver the correct output, then send the correct commands to assure that it actually delivers the desired output. The programmer has a number of parameters to consider, including the following:

1. Type of waveform (e.g., sine, square, triangle, pulse)

2. Frequency

3. Amplitude

4. DC offset

5. Symmetry

6. Modulation

7. Sweep mode

8. Burst mode

The designer must also ensure that the generator is properly terminated. Otherwise, reflections and mismatches could cause output errors or signal degradation.

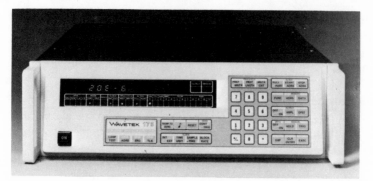

Fig. 3-3 Wavetek 175 Arbitrary Waveform Generator. This generator provides both fixed and customized waveforms under control of an internal microprocessor. *(Courtesy of Wavetek, Inc.)*

A number of programmable function generators are available for use in ATE. Fig. 3-3 shows a Wavetek 175 programmable Arbitrary Waveform Generator, which has capabilities that exceed those of the average function generator. It provides a number of the fixed waveforms found in most function generators, such as sine, square, triangle, ramp. One can adjust the open-circuit output amplitude at any point from 2 mV to 20 V and dc offset from +10 to −10 V with three-digit resolution. One can enter these parameters through the front panel keys, or the controller can set up the generator over the GPIB.

The 175 also allows one to enter the change-of-slope parameters of a customized waveform into four RAMs from the front panel keyboard or over the GPIB. An internal microprocessor connects the data points into a complete waveform. One can also insert four PROMs and call up preprogrammed waveforms. A user can thus maintain a library of PROMs with often-used waveforms.

Once the waveform parameters have been entered, the front panel keys or the GPIB can call up the desired output waveform. The basic capability allows one to generate any waveform that can be plotted on a 256 by 255 data grid. The PROMs or RAMs can be stacked to increase the resolution from 256 to 1024 data points. One can select either smoothed or unsmoothed output, again through the front panel or GPIB. Fig. 3-4 illustrates some of the possible waveforms.

The stepping time from data point to data point can be programmed from 200 ns for fixed waveforms and PROM-stored data points and 500 ns for RAM points up to a total of 999.9 s. The output rate for a 256-word block can be selected from 19.5 kHz to 3.9 μHz (71 h/cycle).

Four operational modes are available. In Continuous mode, the generator oscillates continuously. In Preset Triggered mode, a front panel key, a TTL pulse at the rear panel connector, or a GPIB message will trigger the gen-

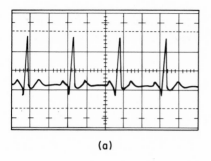

(a)

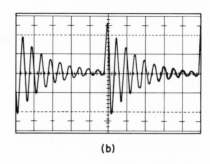

(b)

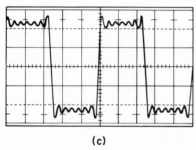

(c)

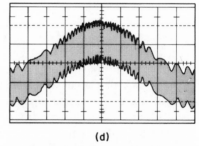

(d)

Fig. 3-4 Examples of waveforms that can be programmed into the 175. Waveform (a) simulates a heartbeat of an EKG. Waveform (b) is a simulated impulse shock. Waveform (c) is a Fourier function. Waveform (d) is a simulated VOR signal. *(Courtesy of Wavetek, Inc.)*

erator, which will output a preset number of cycles (9 to 9999) of the desired waveform. In Monitor Triggered mode, the generator runs continuously from the time it receives a trigger until it receives a hold command. In Hold Control, the generator will stop the output asynchronously with the reference clock. In Ramp-to-Zero mode, the generator steps the output linearly to 0 V.

The 175 has the following GPIB subset capabilities. (One may want to refer to Chap. 2 and Appendix A in order to understand them.)

• Listener (AH1 and L4)

• Talker (SH1 and T6)

• Service Request (SR1)

• Remote/Local (RL1)

• Device Clear (DC1)

• Device Trigger (DT1)

The handshake rate is 2 μs per character in command mode and 220 μs per character in data mode. The 175 has a data storage capacity of 80 characters.

Power Supplies

Since power supplies can provide both operating power and logic signals to the UUT, ATE systems use them extensively. After the test program has set up the output voltage or current, it may connect the power supply output through the switching system to the DMM, then adjust the output still closer to the desired value. This can allow the program to set an inaccurate power supply closer to the desired value. One should be careful of the effects of changing loads and readjust each time the load changes enough to affect the output.

Constant Voltage and Constant Current   Power supplies have a number of useful features for the designer and user. One capability of many power supplies is the constant voltage–constant current feature, which allows it to operate as either a constant voltage or constant current source. The mode in which a power supply operates will depend on operator settings of the controls and the circuit conditions. With constant voltage mode, one selects a regulated output voltage, then sets a current limit, above which the output current will never rise. With constant current mode, the operator selects a regulated current, then sets a voltage limit. An automatic crossover from one to another will occur when the following condition is satisfied:

$$R_{\text{load}} = \frac{\text{voltage setting}}{\text{current setting}}$$

In constant voltage mode, the numerator of the above is the constant voltage output while the denominator is the selected current limit. In constant current mode, the numerator is the voltage limit while the denominator is the constant current.

The crossover point is illustrated in the graph of Fig. 3-5. E_{reg} is the value of voltage selected for constant voltage operation. I_{reg} is the current limit. In constant current operation, the roles are reversed, with the value of E_{reg} being the voltage limit. Let us first consider the portion of the graph that relates to constant voltage operation. Note that at the point where $I_o = 0$, R_L will equal infinity and the output voltage will equal E_{reg}.

As R_L decreases from infinity toward the point x, the voltage will remain constant and the current will increase in reaction to the decreased resistance. When $R_L = E_{\text{reg}}/I_{\text{reg}}$, the output current has reached the limit set by the operator. This point is x on the graph.

Past point x the current cannot increase, since it is limited by the power supply circuitry. As the resistance of the load decreases past its value at x,

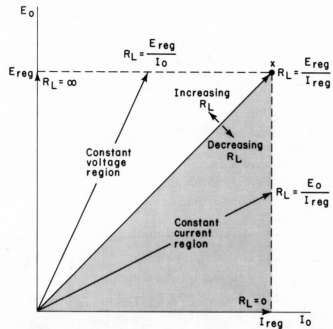

Fig. 3-5 Graph illustrating constant voltage and constant current operation of a power supply. To the left of x, the power supply operates in constant voltage mode, in which output voltage remains constant and current varies with the load. Below x, the power supply operates in the constant current mode, in which current remains constant and voltage varies with the load.

the voltage must decrease in order to maintain a constant current. The load values shown in the shaded region cause the power supply to operate in a constant current mode while those in the unshaded region result in a constant voltage mode of operation. Note that the supply can switch from one mode to the other if the load resistance is varied through x.

Error Sensing The output current that a power supply provides causes a voltage drop in the lines that connect its output to a remote load. This voltage drop subtracts from the voltage at the power supply output and causes an error at the load. Fig. 3-6 illustrates this situation.

Power supplies use *remote error sensing* to correct for this error. The operator connects the power supply's sense inputs to the load, as shown in Fig. 3-6. The sensing circuit determines the error that exists at the load with respect to the desired voltage at the output. The power supply will raise its voltage enough to compensate for the losses.

In the example shown, the 0.5-Ω load connects to the power supply through 0.05 Ω of connecting lead resistance. Although the test program

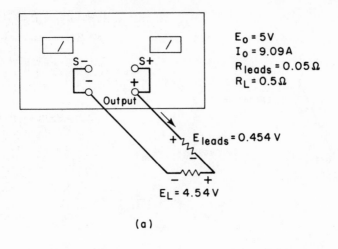

$E_0 = 5\,V$
$I_0 = 9.09\,A$
$R_{leads} = 0.05\,\Omega$
$R_L = 0.5\,\Omega$

$E_{leads} = 0.454\,V$

$E_L = 4.54\,V$

(a)

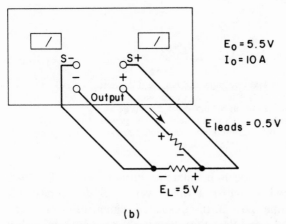

$E_0 = 5.5\,V$
$I_0 = 10\,A$

$E_{leads} = 0.5\,V$

$E_L = 5\,V$

(b)

Fig. 3-6 Illustration of remote error sensing to correct for drops in leads and connections. In (a), the designer requires 5 V at the load, but since the power supply itself provides 5 V, the drop in connecting lines results in a load voltage of 4.54 V. In (b), the use of remote error sensing will result in a steady 5 V at the load.

set the output to 5 V, the loss in the line subtracts from this voltage and only 4.54 V appears at the load. With remote sensing, the power supply output voltage rises to 5.5 V, which provides 5 V to the load.

Another method of correcting for this error is to measure the voltage at the load rather than the power supply output. The program can then adjust the output voltage until the load voltage is corrected. This would require connections from the switching system to each load of interest.

Remote Programming Most power supplies allow remote programming of output voltage or current. One can apply a signal to the programming input of the power supply and vary its output by varying the input signal. The most common parameters for control of power supply output are variable resistance, current, and voltage. In each case, a direct relationship exists between the input parameter and the output signal. With resistance programming, for example, the output voltage is related to the programming resistance as follows:

$$V_{out} = \frac{R_P}{N}$$

N is a constant that depends on the characteristics of the power supplies and is provided in the manufacturer's operating instructions. A typical value for N is 1000 Ω/V.

Another common method of programming voltage and current is voltage programming. A relationship exists between the input control voltage and the output voltage that will be obtained. Common values are ± 10 and ± 1 V, which give a $\pm$ full scale output.

Protection Most power supplies have some type of protection, either for itself or its load. A number of supplies are short circuit-proof and can operate indefinitely with an overload. Of course, the automatic crossover into the constant current or constant voltage modes assures that the power supply will never provide more voltage or current than the operator or test program selected, even when the output is opened or short-circuited. One may want to refer back to Fig. 3-5 to observe that the maximum voltage and current are E_{reg} and I_{reg}.

A method of load protection is the crowbar overprotection circuit. This circuitry shuts down the power supply if the output exceeds a present voltage level. This feature is especially useful if the load consists of voltage-sensitive components. If the series transistor of the power supply develops even a partial short circuit, for example, the rectified output will appear directly at the output and could damage a sensitive load.

Fig. 3-7 shows an example of a crowbar protection circuit. The crowbar protection amplifier, U2, monitors the difference between the preset crowbar reference voltage and the power supply output. When the voltage rises above the reference, the amplifier output fires the SCR (silicon-controlled rectifier), which short-circuits the output, dropping the output to 0. The operator must reset the power supply in some way to restore the output.

Kepco BOP Power Supply Fig. 3-8 shows a Kepco BOP 50-8M Power Supply, which provides an output of ± 50 V, ± 8 A. The power supply allows control of both current and voltage and features automatic crossover

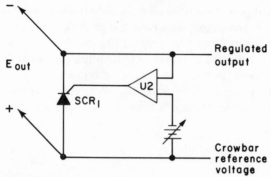

Fig. 3-7 Use of a crowbar protection circuit for load protection. If E_{out} exceeds a preset value, the SCR will conduct and drop the output to 0.

between constant voltage and constant current operation. To program output voltage or current, one applies a signal at the voltage or current programming input binding posts. A ± 10-V signal will control the $\pm$ full scale output of the power supply.

One can also control the power supply over a bus. A plug-in card or a separate programmer will allow remote control over either the IEEE-488 bus or a parallel data bus. The programming of this bus control will be covered in a later chapter on ATE software.

Racal-Dana 1515 Delay Pulse Generator

The timing of the various operations in ATE may best be handled by a device that specializes in timing control. The 1515 Delay Pulse Generator

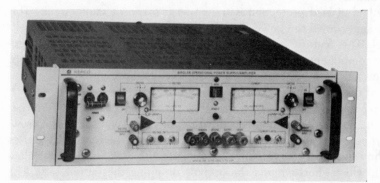

Fig. 3-8 Kepco BOP 50-8M Power Supply. Note the voltage and current programming input terminals and the two sense terminals. In this instance, the sense terminals connect directly to the output terminals. This connection will allow the power supply to operate but will be unable to correct for drops in the leads connected to the load. The voltage and current limit adjustments allow the operator to set up the protection circuitry. *(Courtesy of Kepco, Inc.)*

Fig. 3-9 Racal-Dana Series 1500 Delay Pulse Generator, which can provide timing control of ATE systems. *(Courtesy of Racal-Dana Instruments, Inc.)*

is an example of such a device. The 1515 can operate as a GPIB timing generator to provide timing for ATE measurements. The 1515 is shown in Fig. 3-9. An ATE system that uses the generator is shown in Fig. 3-10. Note that the 1515 provides trigger and gating signals to the devices in the ATE. It can thus control the time at which the devices operate.

Fig. 3-11 illustrates a number of capabilities of the 1515. It can provide an output pulse delayed by 100 ns to 1 s after receipt of a trigger. (The programmable delay actually begins with the output of a marker pulse that occurs less than 100 ns after the trigger). The 1515 can also control the

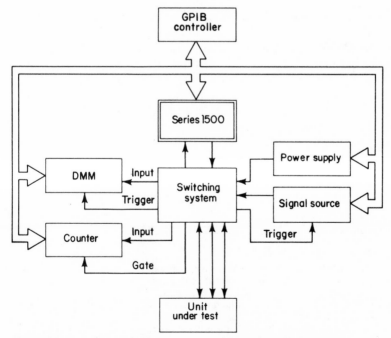

Fig. 3-10 ATE system utilizing the Series 1500 Delay Pulse Generator for trigger and gating signals. *(Courtesy of Racal-Dana Instruments, Inc.)*

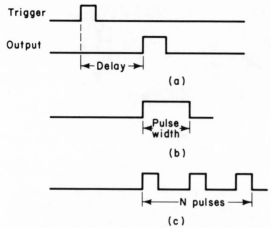

Fig. 3-11 Summary of Delay Pulse Generator capabilities. In (a), the generator provides a pulse delayed for a selectable period after a trigger. The width of the pulse (b) and number of pulses (c) are also selectable. (Couresy of Racal-Dana Instruments, Inc.)

width of the output pulse from 100 ns to 1 s. In its burst mode, it can output a burst of 1 to 9999 pulses for each trigger.

Fig. 3-12 shows a number of applications of the 1515. With a frequency counter, for example, the 1515 can pick out one pulse in a pulse stream and measure the period of that pulse only. It can also gate the counter to count the number of pulses in a particular burst out of a stream of bursts.

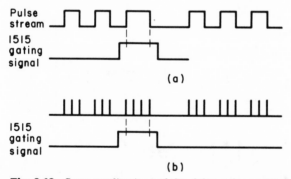

Fig. 3-12 Some applications of the delay pulse generator. In (a), one can program the output signal so it gates a frequency counter at a particular time and for a particular interval. One can thus pick out a single pulse in a stream for period measurement. In (b), the generator gates the counter to count a particular burst of pulses in a stream of pulse bursts. (Courtesy of Racal-Dana Instruments, Inc.)

The 1515 contains a 6802 microprocessor that performs various "smart" functions and maintains the real-time clock and time-code generator. The real-time clock can initiate SRQ interrupts to the controller at specified intervals to initiate various measurement sequences. The real-time clock can thus perform system timing functions for ATE systems that utilize a controller without such timing capability.

The time-code generator will output time of day in one of two formats, either DD:HH:MM:SS or the ATLAS-compatible format DDHH.MMSS. (ATLAS is a high-level language for test systems. It will be covered in a later chapter.) The time-code generator could be used in ATE whose controller lacks such a capability. The controller can read the time code in over the GPIB, then print out the time of each measurement on the test record.

MEASURING INSTRUMENTS

Measuring instruments perform measurements at the UUT output, at a test node, across a device, or at the output of a stimulus. The latter method allows accurate setup of the stimulus output. If a particular test requires a precise audio signal level, for example, the controller will send the commands to set up the audio generator for that signal level. Because of load and instrument variations, however, the output may deviate somewhat from the value that the controller commanded. The controller can fine-tune the output as follows:

1. Command the switching system to connect the audio generator output to the DMM input and to its load.

2. Set up the DMM to measure ac volts.

3. Read in the voltage from the DMM.

4. Calculate the difference between the desired and actual outputs and determine the required correction.

5. Adjust the generator to the corrected value.

6. Repeat the process until the output lines are within acceptable limits.

One must consider a number of factors when selecting measuring instruments for use in ATE. A few of the considerations are as follows:

1. The input range must be adequate for measurement of all parameters of interest. A frequency counter, for example, may have to measure a frequency higher than one might expect after a cursory study. An ATE stimulus may provide an input frequency of 10 MHz, so one might expect

that a counter with that frequency response would be adequate. If the UUT has frequency multipliers, however, the user may find that the UUT measurement requirements lie far outside of the counter's capability.

2. The capabilities must cover all required measurements. Most DMMs, for example, measure dc volts, ac volts, and resistance. If a UUT requires a measurement of dc current, the DMM must also have this capability. A counter may require a special plug-in to measure the time interval of a signal, so the user must either obtain this plug-in along with the counter or use a counter that has the capability included.

3. The accuracy of each function and range must match the requirements of the UUT. A general rule is that the measuring device should have an accuracy a number of times (preferably 10) better than the highest UUT accuracy required. If a test requires a UUT RF power output of 100 mW at an accuracy of ±1 percent, then the power meter that makes the measurement should have an accuracy of 0.1 percent. One should also assure that all measuring devices are properly terminated. Otherwise, a mismatch could cause erroneous readings. The subject of accuracy and uncertainty of measurements will be covered in detail in a later chapter.

A variety of measuring devices exist for use in ATE. Among the most common are the DMM, electronic counter, power meter, waveform analyzer, spectrum analyzer, analog to digital converter, and oscilloscope. The sensor used in ICTs to measure digital signals at board nodes has been covered. Some of the other devices will be covered in this section.

Digital Multimeter

Digital multimeters commonly have the capability of performing dc and ac volts and two-wire resistance measurements. This basic DMM is found in a number of ATE systems. A number of DMMs also have the capability of performing four-wire resistance measurements. An advantage of the four-wire measurement over two-wire is that the four-wire measurement avoids much of the error that results from the measurement of lead resistance.

The resistance measured in a two-wire measurement includes that of the leads that connect the resistance to the DMM input. The four-wire method utilizes a current source and voltage measurement. The current source provides a known current through the resistance. The voltmeter measures the voltage directly across the resistance. The result (voltage divided by current) will be essentially independent of the lead resistance. This measurement is shown in Fig. 3-13.

DMMs have a number of selectable ranges (e.g., 0.2, 2, 20, 200 V) as well as an autorange that senses the input level and selects the correct range.

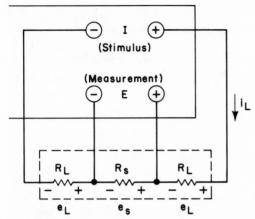

Fig. 3-13 Four-lead resistance mesurement. The measured voltage across the load (e_s) divided by a constant current (i_L) gives the value of R_s. This method minimizes the errors caused by voltage drops in the connecting leads (represented by e_L).

A disadvantage of autorange is that it may operate slower than the direct setting of range. This will slow down the test and could affect production if the test requires many measurements. A bad reading could also occur if the DMM sends the measurement to the controller before the DMM settles. A number of DMMs wait until the reading has settled before sending it over the bus.

Racal-Dana 5004 Digital Multimeter   Fig. 3-14 shows the 5004, a three-function DMM. The 5004 measures dc volts in five ranges from 0.1 to 1000 V, with an accuracy as high as $\pm(0.007\% + 3$ digits$)$. It also measures resistance in six ranges, from 100 Ω to 10 MΩ, and true RMS ac voltage in

Fig. 3-14   Racal-Dana 5004 Digital Multimeter. This "smart" DMM contains a microprocessor for computations and control and RAM storage for up to 120 readings. The 5004 can also store up to 10 reading measurement setups, then call them up when the operator requests it through front panel controls or the controller requests one over the GPIB. *(Courtesy of Racal-Dana Instruments Inc.)*

four ranges from 1 to 750 V. The 5004 contains a microprocessor that performs a number of "smart" functions including the following:

Null: This push button stores the present reading as a zero offset. An operator can thus nullify such factors as thermal voltages and lead resistance.

Offset: This function allows a constant to be stored from the 5004 keyboard and added to or subtracted from all future measurements.

Percent Deviation: This function allows one to compute $(x - c)/c \times 100$, where x is the measured value and c is a stored constant.

LAH: With this function, the 5004 stores the highest, lowest, and average readings in a series of measurements. One can recall these values from the front panel or the controller can read them over the GPIB. A low peak, high peak, or average mode can also be selected. The 5004 will update the display or output data to the GPIB only when it detects a new peak or average value. The controller can send a simple GPIB command to trigger an averaging sequence or peak mode, then perform other functions until it receives an SRQ from the 5004 that a value is available.

Time: With this function, the 5004 can operate "offline" under control of its internal 96-h clock. The 5004 can control the timing of a lengthy measurement sequence, as shown in Fig. 3-15.

Buffer Memory: The 5004 contains RAM storage for up to 120 readings. One can combine this capability with the time function to achieve unattended operation over a period of time. At the end of the sequence, the operator or controller can read the accumulated measurement data.

The buffer memory can also store up to 10 measurement setups, which the operator can then call up from the front panel or the controller can initiate with a two-character program command over GPIB. This capability allows one to store the measurement setups at the beginning of a test and implement them as needed throughout the test.

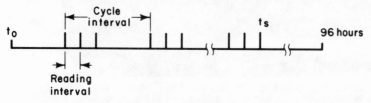

Fig. 3-15 Example of offline operation of the 5004 DMM. The 5004 can operate under control of its 96-h clock to take readings at various intervals in each cycle. *(Courtesy of Racal-Dana Instruments Inc.)*

The 5004 has the capability of being calibrated without making any internal adjustments. To calibrate the 5004, one need only select the calibration mode, connect an accurate standard to the input, then press the appropriate controls to correct for errors. The 5004 stores all calibration constants in a nonvolatile memory. An automatic calibration system can substitute GPIB commands for the front panel operations.

Electronic Counter

Fig. 3-16 shows a block diagram for an electronic counter set up to measure frequency. The basic accuracy of the counter derives from the accuracy of the time-base oscillator, which controls the gate time of the counter. The gate opens for a specified period and passes a number of cycles of the input frequency, which the counters count.

Electronic counters measure more than frequency. A number of them also measure the following parameters:

1. Period

2. Time interval, the time between two events, such as a start or stop signal or two points on a waveform. The concept of time interval is illustrated in Fig. 3-17.

3. Totalize, during which the counter counts the total number of cycles of an input signal, rather than the number of cycles per second. The operator can use a front panel switch to open and close the gate. In some counters, an input signal will also control the gate.

4. Ratio, in which one signal controls the gate while the counter counts the higher frequency signal. The result is the ratio between the two signal

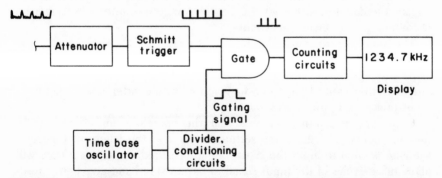

Fig. 3-16 Block diagram of an electronic counter set up to measure frequency. The attenuator and Schmitt trigger condition the input signal and apply it to the gate. The timing signal is also an input to the gate. The gated output is counted in the counting circuits and displayed.

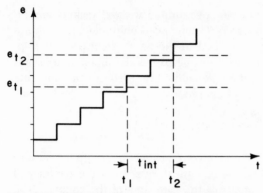

Fig. 3-17 Example of a time interval measurement. The operator sets two thresholds, e_{t1} and e_{t2}, both with positive slope. At t_1, the signal level exceeds e_{t1} in a positive direction, so the counter begins its count. At t_2, the signal crosses the e_{t2} level and the counter stops counting. The display gives the time interval, $t_2 - t_1$.

frequencies. Some counters measure other parameters, such as RF pulse rate and width.

A number of counter functions must be set up in order to make the desired measurement. First, one must select the type of measurement to be made (frequency, period, time interval, etc.). The input coupling switch selects whether ac or dc coupling will be used. The trigger level must be set to the point where the counter measures correctly. The trigger level control adjusts the hysteresis level of the Schmitt trigger circuit in Fig. 3-16 to the point where the counter triggers at the correct point on the waveform. If the hysteresis level is set too high, the input signal cannot trigger the counter. If the level is set too low, the counter will trigger on noise and give an erroneous count.

The slope control must also be set to match the characteristics of the waveform to be measured. The + slope indicates that a signal with a positive slope (i.e., going in a positive direction) will trigger the Schmitt trigger circuit. Other controls that one may adjust include attenuation, measurement range, and input impedance.

Gate time is another variable that the operator can set with some measurements. The gate-time setting determines the length of time that the gate is open to input the signal being measured. A long gate time will allow more cycles of the input signal to be measured and give better resolution. It could also result in a slower measurement rate. A shorter gate time may give a higher measurement rate but a lower resolution.

Fig. 3-18 Hewlett-Packard model 5345A Electronic Counter with HP5355A Automatic Frequency Converter plug-in installed. The 5356B Frequency Converter Head allows frequency measurements to 26 GHz. (*Courtesy of Hewlett-Packard Company.*)

Fig. 3-18 shows the Hewlett-Packard 5345A Electronic Counter with a 5355A plug-in installed. Frequency measurement capability ranges from 50 μHz to 500 MHz. Time interval ranges from 10 ns to 20,000 s, with a resolution of 2 ns. The gate time is controllable from 100 ns to 1000 s in decade steps. Sensitivity, the minimum signal that can be counted, is 20 mV RMS for sine waves and 50 mV peak-to-peak for pulses.

The 5345A has two options. Option 011 provides bus control of the front panel, with the exception of triggering slope and level control. HP recommends this option for a benchtop calculator-controlled environment. Option 012 is similar to 011, but it has the additional capability of trigger slope and level control. HP recommends this option for computer-controlled situations.

A number of plug-ins are available to extend the range and capability of the 5345A. Fig. 3-18 shows the 5355A plug-in installed in the counter. The 5355A provides pulsed and continuous wave frequency capability up to 40 GHz, if it is used with the proper frequency converter head. It can measure pulsed signals as narrow as 60 ns and even lower with external gating.

The 5355A utilizes internal microprocessor control for automatic operation and diagnostic routines. The front panel controls work in conjunction with the microprocessor to define offsets. An *mx + b* offset mode is also included for the testing of receivers. The local oscillator is measured directly, then the result is multiplied by the appropriate harmonic number. This is offset by the receiver IF (intermediate frequency) on the counter to obtain a display of tuned receiver frequency.

Oscilloscopes

An oscilloscope is an example of a measuring device that operates in many ATE systems without the advantage of GPIB control. The controller usually sends a request to the display to prompt the operator to observe the waveform at a particular node and measure the required characteristics. The controller could display the following message:

MEASURE RISE TIME AT TP 221

The operator will measure the rise time, as requested, then press a key to continue the program. The controller may then display:

ENTER RISE TIME

The operator will enter the rise time and the program will use the value in its calculations.

Such a process is time-consuming and may raise the requirements for the technical capabilities of the operator. The ideal solution would be to automate these measurements also.

A number of oscilloscopes now interface with the GPIB to make certain measurements and pass the results to the controller. The Tektronix 468 Digital Storage Oscilloscope shown in Fig. 3-19 is such an oscilloscope. It

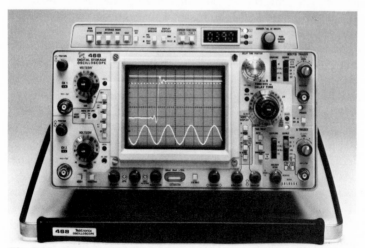

Fig. 3-19 Tektronix 468 Digital Storage Oscilloscope. The 468 can store two 512-word waveforms or four 256-word waveforms. As an addressable talker, it can pass the stored values over the GPIB. (*Courtesy of Tektronix, Inc.*)

can digitize and display 10 MHz one-shot events and store up to two 512-word waveforms or four 256-word waveforms. It is an addressable talker and can pass the stored waveform over the GPIB upon command from the controller.

Tektronix 7D20 Programmable Digitizer The 7D20 allows the owners of most Tektronix 7000-series oscilloscopes to use them as programmable digital oscilloscopes. Fig. 3-20 shows the 7D20 installed in a Tektronix 7603 Oscilloscope. The 7D20 has 1024 points of storage for each of six waveforms, as well as a reference waveform. It can simultaneously acquire two channels at a time. The two input channels contain dedicated analog to digital converters. One can recall any of the six stored waveforms and display them in any of the formats available (Y-T, X-Y, Expanded, Compressed).

Six front panel setups can be stored in a nonvolatile EAROM (electrically-alterable ROM), then recalled as one desires. The store and recall capabilities are controllable through menus.

The 7D20 is also GPIB-programmable. It can receive and transmit text messages, waveforms, and front panel settings. One can activate controller

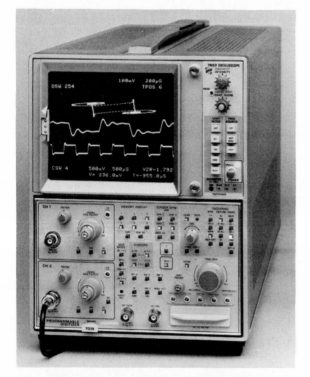

Fig. 3-20 Tektronix 7D20 Programmable Digitizer installed in a 7603 Oscilloscope. *(Courtesy of Tektronix, Inc.)*

programs by pressing the Identify button on a probe. This capability allows measurements at some distance from the oscilloscope.

SWITCHING SYSTEM

The easiest switching system to imagine is probably a rotary switch, which manual test sets may use to connect UUT test points to measurement devices and stimuli. A relay would form the simplest programmable switching system. In fact, switching systems often consist of a number of such relays. The input and output connections will vary with the type of system. Fig. 3-21 shows some types of switching systems. Fig. 3-22 shows the Racal-Dana 1200 switching system.

Some switching systems connect any number of inputs to one output at a time. One coaxial scanner has 100 pins that can connect to any one of four channels. The user can connect a number of UUT test points to the pins, then connect a power meter to one channel, a DMM to another, a frequency counter to another, etc. The controller can then command the connection of one of the test points to a measurement device at one of the outputs.

Another switching system connects any one of 192 inputs to up to five

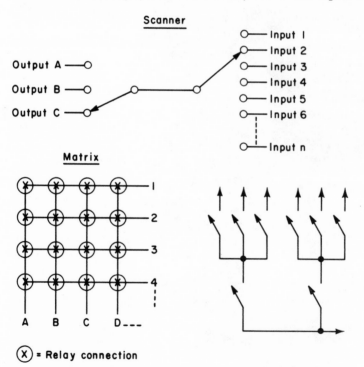

(X) = Relay connection

Fig. 3-21 Examples of switching systems. The scanner connects one input to one output. The matrix connects a number of inputs to the outputs.

Fig. 3-22 Racal-Dana 1200 Switching System.

outputs simultaneously. The advantage of this system over the one mentioned above is that a number of devices can connect simultaneously to a test point. The controller can connect a frequency counter and a distortion analyzer to the same test point at the same time.

Fig. 3-23 shows the block diagram of the Autek FX-30 Dual 4 × 100

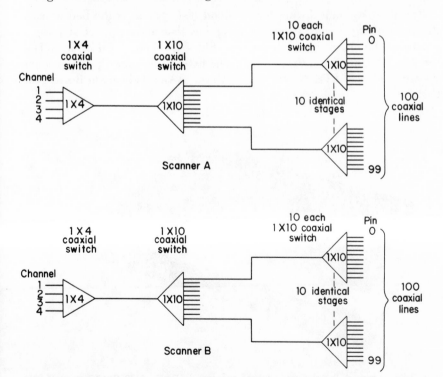

Fig. 3-23 Block diagram of the Autek FX-30 Dual 4 × 100 Coaxial Scanner. Any one of 100 inputs in each scanner section can connect to any one of four outputs. (*Courtesy of Autek Systems Corp.*)

Coaxial Scanner. The FX30 is similar to the scanner above except that the FX30 consists of two independent scanners, each of 100 pins. Each scanner will connect any one of 100 pins to any one of four channels under GPIB control. The capability exists to program either a single connection or a multipoint scan through a number of pins. In the latter mode, the test program sets the first and last pins, then triggers the scanner to select each pin in order at a rate selected by a front panel control. A later chapter will cover the message format and programming of the FX30.

FIXTURES

The test fixture provides the ATE system with an electrical and mechanical interface with the UUT. In some instances, the fixture may take the form of a cable that runs from the ATE system to the UUT connector. In functional ATE systems, the edge connector may serve as the equivalent of a test fixture. Organizations that build ATE systems in-house can either build their own fixtures or purchase them from a manufacturer that specializes in fixtures.

The most common fixture for in-circuit test systems is the bed of nails fixture, which contains a number of probes that make contact at various points on the circuit board under test. Fig. 3-24 shows a fixture manufactured by Virginia Panel Corporation. The fixture has been wired for use on the GenRad 2270 ATE System. Fig. 3-25 shows GenRad Circuit Board Test Systems.

Fig. 3-24 Virginia Panel Corp. Fixture for use on GenRad 2270 ATE System. (*Courtesy of Virginia Panel Corp.*)

Fig. 3-25 GenRad 2270 (*left rear*), 2271 (*right rear*) and 2272 (*front*) Circuit Board Test Systems showing circuit boards under test installed in each fixture. (*Courtesy of GenRad, Inc., Concord, Mass.*)

The test fixture probes make contact with the circuit board test nodes. A probe is shown in Fig. 3-26. The internal spring provides the pressure that gives a positive contact between the probe and the circuit board node. The plunger rides inside the receptacle. The tip that contacts the circuit board forms the top of the plunger. A number of tip styles are available for various applications. Fig. 3-27 and 3-28 show a number of tips and their possible applications. Pointed tips will penetrate oxides and contaminants, while smooth tips avoid indentations. Some tips contact plated-through holes while others are especially designed to contact wire-wrap pins or component leads.

GPIB INTERFACES

A number of devices have appeared on the market that perform GPIB interface functions. Semiconductor manufacturers have developed GPIB chips, for example, that handle the interfacing for devices. The use of such chips relieves instrument manufacturers of the need to design special interfaces for their instruments.

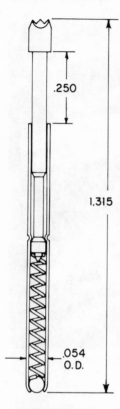

.250

1.315

.054
O.D.

Fig. 3-26 Example of a probe for a bed-of-nails fixture. Tips are available for various applications. The internal spring assures a positive contact between the tip and the board. (*Courtesy of Virginia Panel Corp.*)

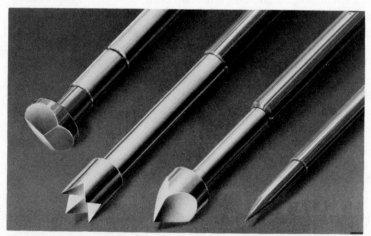

Fig. 3-27 Examples of probe tips. Each tip has a particular application. (*Courtesy of Everett/Charles Contact Products, Inc.*)

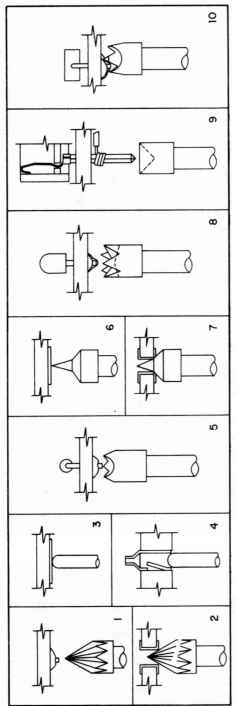

Fig. 3-28 Various styles of probe tips and their uses. (*Courtesy of Virginia Panel Corp.*)

67

A number of products have also appeared that interface the controller and other devices on the GPIB. Again, they make the design of a device for GPIB use a simpler task, as well as a less expensive one. The design engineer can select a product that provides the interfacing and control desired, then include it in the instrument design. The alternative is to design a unique interface circuit, generally a more expensive and time-consuming task. This section will discuss a number of GPIB devices.

Ziatech 7805 GPIB Computer

The 7805 provides an interface between the GPIB, the STD bus, and the RS-232C serial bus. A block diagram is shown in Fig. 3-29. An on-board 8085 microprocessor, 8K bytes of user ROM, and 1K bytes of RAM perform the necessary control functions for the interface. The 7805 can be set to perform as a talker, listener, talker-listener, or a controller. The 7805 can serve as the GPIB control in dedicated test instruments. It can also be used as the GPIB port in "smart" instruments. Two RS-232C ports allow serial communication with other devices.

Intel 8291A GPIB Talker/Listener

The 8291A is a chip used to interface microprocessors to the GPIB. It provides complete talker and listener capabilities, with the following subset interface functions: SH, AH, TE, LE, SR, RL, PP, DC, and DT. The 8291A operates with a clock in the range of 1 to 8 MHz.

An 8293 GPIB Transceiver chip provides the electrical interface between the 8291A and the GPIB. Fig. 3-30 shows the connection of the two devices

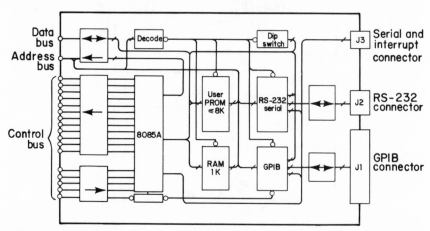

Fig. 3-29 Ziatech 7805 GPIB Computer block diagram. The 7805 provides an interface between the GPIB, STD bus, and the RS-232C serial bus. (*Courtesy of Ziatech Corp.*)

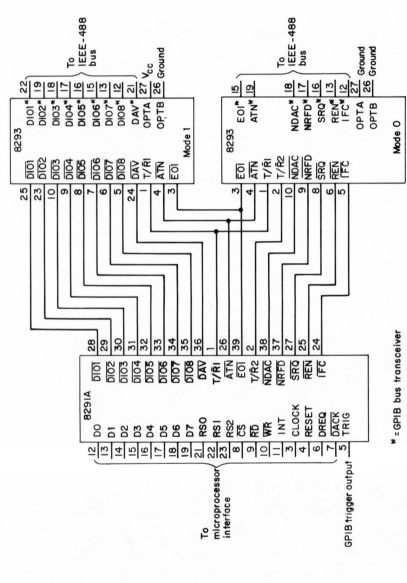

Fig. 3-30 Intel 8291A GPIB Talker/Listener with the 8293 GPIB Transceiver gives an instrument GPIB capability. (*Reprinted by permission of Intel Corporation, Copyright 1980*)

* = GPIB bus transceiver

in a GPIB interface. An instrument designer can thus use the 8291A and 8293 with microprocessor circuitry to give an instrument GPIB capability. At the same time, the microprocessor can be used for other "smart" functions.

ICS Electronics 4885A RS-232 to IEEE-488

The 4885A allows a computer (or timesharing computer system) to utilize an RS-232 I/O port in order to act as an IEEE-488 bus controller. The 4885A accepts the high-level computer commands over the RS-232 and converts them to GPIB universal and addressed commands. It allows the computer to address any device on the bus to send or receive data and performs the appropriate conversion (RS-232 to GPIB or vice versa) on the data, depending on its direction of flow. Fig. 3-31 shows the 4885A.

When ordered by the computer, the 4885A can accept service requests, conduct a serial poll to determine which device requested service, and conduct a parallel poll to obtain the status of the GPIB devices. The 4885A has C1 through C4 and C25 controller subset function capabilities, which include source and acceptor handshakes, single and extended addresses, service requests, interrupts, remote enable, device trigger, and serial and parallel polls.

Fig. 3-32 shows an application of such devices as the 4885A. The computer connects through its RS-232 port to the terminal and 4885A. The 4885A output interfaces with the GPIB, which connects to a frequency

Fig. 3-31 ICS Electronics Corp. 4885A Bus Controller allows control of the IEEE-488 bus from an RS-232C line. (*Courtesy of ICS Electronics Corp.*)

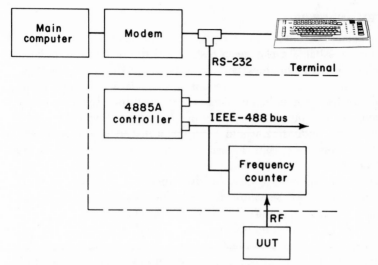

Fig. 3-32 The 4885A connected to a time-shared computer system and the IEEE-488 bus. (*Courtesy of ICS Electronics Corp.*)

counter in the ATE. The frequency counter input connects to the RF output of a UUT. The following is a computer routine that controls the measurement of the frequency of the RF source.

```
Dimension IA (20)
Call Wait (2)
Print 5
5 Format ('-','%WRT 02, 3KMO')
40 Print 6
6 Format ('-','%WRT02,H')
8 Print 7
7 Format ('-','%RED02')
Red 75,IA
```

The first statement dimensions variable IA, which will be used later for the measured value. The wait statement provides a delay. The Print statements place commands on the GPIB. The combination of Print 5 and statement 5 is sent over the GPIB to the counter to initialize it in accordance with the instructions of the manufacturer. Statements 40 and 6 trigger the counter to make a measurement. Statements 8 and 7 together command the 4885A to read in the measured value from the counter over the GPIB and send it to the computer. The final instruction reads in the measured value and assigns it to variable IA. In statement 5, the factor 02 indicates that the GPIB address of the counter is 02.

SIGNATURE ANALYSIS

The emergence of microprocessor circuits, bidirectional buses, and complex LSI circuits necessitated a change in testing and troubleshooting philosophies. Such standard techniques as static tests and guided-probe methods may be inadequate to analyze a bidirectional bus node well enough to determine if it is faulty or is being affected by something else. The use of stored responses, in which the responses of a known-good circuit are compared to the circuit under test, would be impractical. The enormous amount of data that such complex circuits can handle could require enormous memory space in order to perform a thorough check.

ATE system designers have increasingly turned to signature analysis to analyze circuits under test. Signature analysis techniques compress the stream of data into a unique "signature," usually four hexadecimal digits. If the same data passes the same point over the same period, it will have the same signature every time. Fig. 3-33 illustrates a crude method of compressing a stream of data into a signature. The stream of data serves as the clock input to a counter. An enable input starts and stops the counting sequence at the same point each time. To do this, of course, the enable must be derived in some way from the data stream. If the data stream is identical every time, and the enable pulse is the same width and occurs at the same point, the counter output will be the same hexadecimal "signature" every time.

The signature analyzer in an ATE system functions in much the same way, except that it is much more complex. The ATE system can learn the signature at each node of interest on a good board and store the responses in memory. During the test, the ATE system compares the good signatures with those at the nodes of the circuit under test. If they match, the circuit passes. If they differ, the operator can troubleshoot by checking the signatures at other points in the circuit that affect the failed node. If the circuit

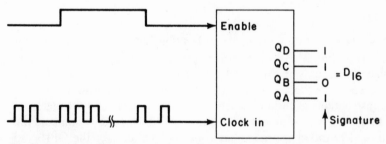

Fig. 3-33 A simplified example of the creation of a signature. The data stream at the clock input increments the counter during the enable pulse. The value at the counter output is the signature of the data stream under the conditions stated.

has a feedback loop, diagnosis and fault localization can still be difficult unless the operator can break the feedback loop.

The signature analyzer requires a stream of data from the circuit under test to obtain a signature. Either the board itself must have such a capability designed into it or the ATE system must apply test patterns to the circuit to exercise all possible states. A number of methods exist to accomplish this. The circuit can be set up to run through all possible patterns. Another method is to apply a stimulus that controls the pattern.

Fig. 3-34*a* shows an example of the latter. A counter is connected to the address bus and allowed to sequence through its entire count. This will output the contents of each addressable word onto the bus, where the signature analyzer can obtain the signature. With another method, the signature analyzer stimulus acts as a program memory for the microprocessor. This method is illustrated in Fig. 3-31*b*. The address drivers connect to the address bus and cycle through their entire count, while the word generator connects to the data bus.

Each node on a board has its own signature. A board with 200 nodes would require as few as 400 bytes for the 200 four-digit hexadecimal signatures.

Two methods of signature analysis are transition counting and pseudo-random binary sequence (PRBS). With transition counting, a counter increments each time a change of state occurs on the node under test. Hewlett-Packard introduced the PRBS technique in 1977 to reduce the probability of errors experienced with transition counting. This method is illustrated in Fig. 3-35, which represents the signature analysis feedback shift register used in the Hewlett-Packard 3060A Board Test System. The circuit sorts the data stream into one of 2^{16} different combinations in the shift register.

Fig. 3-36 shows the state diagram for a 3-bit PRBS generator. In the initial state, the register is set to all 0s, or state 0. The input sequence is clocked serially into the registers.

The state diagram shows that if a logic 1 is applied, the register will change to state $4(100_2)$. A 1 will be clocked into the leftmost cell for the 100_2 count. If a zero is applied, the register will remain in state zero. If the register is in state 4 and another 1 is applied, the register will change to state 2, as shown on the state diagram. The other states can be understood if one remembers that the three-input exclusive-or will produce a 1 output only when one or three of its inputs are 1.

Fig. 3-37 illustrates the advantage of PRBS techniques. Eight different signatures exist for this circuit, which doubles the possibilities of an equivalent transition counter. Note that the signatures begin to repeat only at the fourth bit in the sequence, when the number of bits in the bit stream exceed the number of cells in the register.

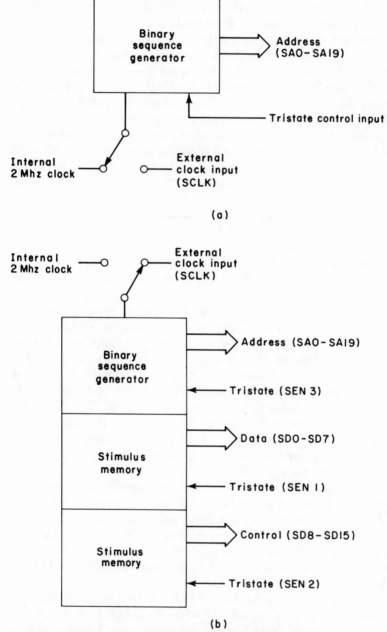

Fig. 3-34 Examples of methods to obtain test patterns for signature analyzers. In (a), a counter connects to an address bus and sequences through its entire count. This will place each addressable word on the bus. In (b), the stimulus acts as program memory. (*Courtesy of Hewlett-Packard Company.*)

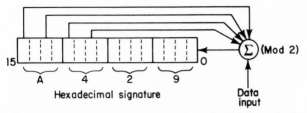

Fig. 3-35 A 16-bit signature analysis feedback register. (*Courtesy of Hewlett-Packard Company.*)

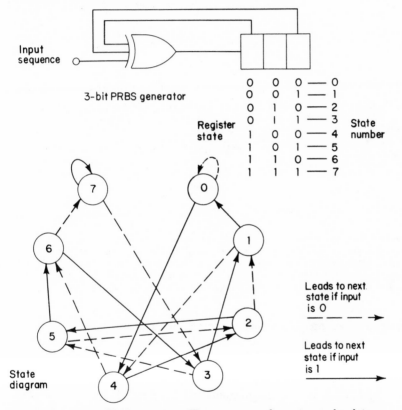

Fig. 3-36 A 3-bit PRBS generator. The sequence of events can be determined by using the present state and the value of the next input to project the next state. (*Reprinted with permission from Electronic Design, vol. 28, no. 3; copyright Hayden Publishing Co., Inc., 1980.*)

With such a large number of possible combinations, $(2^{16}$ for a 16-bit register), the circuit will respond to any change in the data stream. It will produce a different signature for all single-bit errors and all but one out of 2^{16} multibit errors, which gives it a 99.98 percent probability of detecting an error in the data stream.

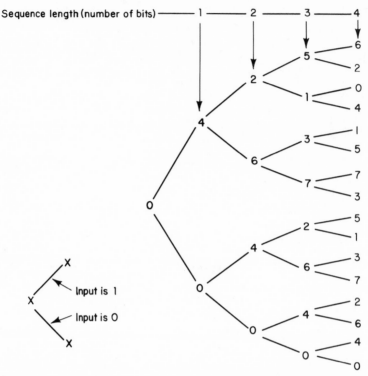

Fig. 3-37 The signature tree of the PRBS generator of Fig. 3-36. Note that compression (i.e., signatures repeat) occurs only after the sequence is longer than the register. With a transition counter, compression occurs much earlier for a higher probability of error. (*Reprinted with permission from Electronic Design, vol. 28, no. 3; copyright Hayden Publishing Co., Inc., 1980.*)

HEWLETT-PACKARD 5005B SIGNATURE MULTIMETER

The HP5005 shown in Fig. 3-38 is an example of the instruments that have appeared on the market since the introduction of signature analysis. It performs signature analysis up to 25 MHz. The 5005B has a 100 percent probability of detecting single-bit errors and a 99.998 percent chance of detecting multiple-bit errors.

The HP5005B Timing Pod has connections for Start, Stop, and Clock signal inputs. The Start and Stop signals enable the measurement sequence. One can select either the rising or falling edge of the Clock, Start, and Stop signals to control the sequence. The operator connects these signals, selects the polarities, then touches the data probe to the node of interest. The display will give the four-digit hexadecimal signature, which the operator can check against the characteristics of a known-good node. The presence of a flashing Gate light indicates that the signature at the node is stable. A

Fig. 3-38 Hewlett-Packard 5005 Signature Multimeter being used for checking signatures on a circuit board. (*Courtesy of Hewlett-Packard Company.*)

flashing Unstable light indicates that a difference exists between two successive signatures.

The display uses the characters 0 to 9 and ACFHPU for the hexadecimal digits. Hewlett-Packard chose the uncharacteristic upper hexadecimal digits for a number of reasons. If they had used the standard hexadecimal digits (ABCDEF) for the seven-segment display, for example, a B would have looked like an 8 and a 0 would have looked like a D.

The HP5005B can be set to operate with present threshold levels for TTL, CMOS, and ECL logic families. The front panel controls allow one to adjust the levels from $+12.5$ to -12.5 V to cover other logic families.

In addition to its signature analysis capability, the HP5005B contains a dc voltmeter, ohmmeter, and differential voltage measurement capability. A voltage threshold capability provides a method to measure the high and low levels of dynamic signals. A counter capability allows totalizing and frequency measurement to 50 MHz and time interval to a resolution of 100 ns.

REFERENCES

Bahr, Dennis: "Understanding Signature Analysis," *Electronics Test*, Nov. 1982.

Conway, Arch: "DMM Sets the Pace in Low Cost ATE," *Electronic Design*, Sept. 1, 1980, pp. 101–106.

Dynamic Digital Board Testing, Application Note 308-1, Hewlett-Packard, Nov. 1980.

Fundamentals of the Electronic Counters, Application Note 200, Hewlett-Packard, July 1978.

Glau, Gordon: "Trends in Probe Applications," *Circuits Manufacturing,* Aug. 1981.

Grappel, Robert D., and Jack Hemenway: "EDN Software Tutorial: Pseudorandom Generators," *EDN,* May 20, 1980, pp. 119–123.

Guidelines for Signature Analysis, Application Note 222-4, Hewlett-Packard, Jan. 1981, pp. 2–23.

Humphrey, John R., and Kamram Firooz: "ATE Brings Speedy, Complete Testing via Signature Analysis," *Electronic Design,* Feb. 1, 1980, pp. 78–79.

Javetski, John: "STD Bus Cards Pack More Punch," *Electronic Products,* May 11, 1982, pp. 79–87.

Jessen, Ken: "In-Circuit Tester Answers μP-board Challenge," *Electronic Design,* Nov. 8, 1980, pp. 97–101.

Kubert, Vincent, and Peter Seuffert: "Test Fixture Selection Criteria," *Electronics Test,* introductory issue, 1978.

Laengrich, Norbert: "Instrument Intelligence Determines 488 Bus Speed," *Electronic Design,* Oct. 15, 1981, pp. 181–185.

Levasseur, Daniel: "Simplify IEEE-488 Implementation with a Multifunction Interface," *EDN,* Mar. 5, 1979, pp. 105–113.

Madni, Asad M., and Stanley M. Wolf: "ATE: Trends in Communications/Microwave Test Instruments," *Military Electronics/Countermeasures,* June 1982, pp. 15–18.

Raymond, Douglas W.: "In-Circuit Testing Comes of Age," *Computer Design,* Aug. 1981, pp. 117–124.

Runyon, Stan: "BASIC Underlies the Multiple Language of Smart Instruments," *Electronic Design,* Oct. 11, 1979, pp. 95–98.

Santoni, Andy: "IEEE-488-Compatible Instruments," *EDN,* Nov. 5, 1979, pp. 91–98.

Skilling, James K.: "Signatures Take a Circuit's Pulse by Transition Counting or PRBS—But Watch Those Loops," *Electronic Design,* Feb. 1, 1980, pp. 65–68.

Tilden, Mark, and Bob Ramirez: "Understanding IEEE-488 Basics Simplifies System Integration," *EDN,* June 9, 1982, pp. 121–129.

Urdaneta, Nelson: "Keeping Fast Tests on a Tight Schedule," *Electronics,* Aug. 14, 1980, pp. 111–115.

Williams, Ronald M.: "LSI Chips Ease Standard 488 Bus Interfacing," *Computer Design,* Oct. 1979, pp. 123–131.

4

THE
CONTROLLER

ATE system activities center around the controller. As was discussed in Chap. 1, the controller dominates the test cycle and controls all information that passes over the bus. Among its functions in ATE are the following:

1. *Management of the test cycle:* Under control of the test program, the controller supervises the test cycle and directs the operation of the talker and listeners on the bus. It sets up and begins the handshake routine to transfer data from talker to listener. (Once it does so, the talker and listeners complete the handshake independently without controller intervention. The controller takes over again when the devices complete the cycle.) The controller sends the commands that place the devices in the correct operating modes. It commands the switching system to make the necessary interconnections, the stimuli to provide the outputs to the UUT, and the measuring instruments to make the measurements. It also controls ATE self-test activities.

2. *Data processing:* The controller receives data from the measuring devices and the operator and checks that the inputs are within tolerance. It performs calculations, applies correction factors, and analyzes and reduces data. It may utilize a software package to create the test program from information it receives from a programmer or a sample board known to be good.

3. *Communication with the operator:* The controller provides the operator-machine interface for communication with the operator. After the operator enters the command that starts the test, the controller provides information and requests to the operator as the test proceeds. If the test requires that the operator make a measurement and provide the result,

the controller will send the request to a display, then read in the operator's response from a keyboard or other input device. If the value is out of specification, the controller may enter its diagnostic program and provide guided-probe instructions to the operator that will localize the fault.

4. *Provide test records:* One advantage of ATE over manual systems is that ATE can provide better test records with less effort. With manual test sets, operators must fill out test records by hand. Since manual record keeping is time-consuming and error-prone, organizations either keep them as brief as possible or accept the errors and lost time. ATE systems, on the other hand, generally print out test records automatically. A few lines of simple progam code will provide the required data, headings, summaries, and results. The extra information may take only a few extra seconds of time. If the printer contains a buffer, however, the process could introduce hardly any delay. The ATE system will print out a final test record that is always complete, neat, and essentially error-free. ATE users should nevertheless take care to avoid including extraneous information that is "nice to know" but unessential. Otherwise, the result would be a cluttered printout on which information of significance is buried in the maze of insignificant data.

THE TYPES OF CONTROLLERS

Most ATE controllers fall into one of four categories: minicomputer (or time-shared host computer, perhaps tied in with a modem), microcomputer, desktop calculator, and bus controller. The bus controller's sole function is control of the bus. It is often used in a *cluster* of test equipment on a benchtop for testing and diagnostics, but it can also function as a controller in ATE systems.

The minicomputer and desktop calculator are general-purpose devices that either have bus capability built-in or available as an option. In some cases, the user has to design a bus interface board, but more often nowadays some useful bus capability comes with minicomputers and desktop calculators. The microcomputer may be built into the ATE by the manufacturer and designed and programmed as a dedicated controller.

Controller Capabilities

The variations in devices that can serve as controllers are enormous. The type that one selects for a particular ATE system depends on many factors. The following are some considerations.

Bus Capability The capability of the controller to interface with a bus in order to control and communicate with other devices in the system is a basic one. The type of bus that is chosen will depend on a number of items, including the capabilities of the devices themselves. ATE systems generally use the GPIB to control test equipment, the RS-232C bus to control some peripherals, and a number of other buses to control other activities. Fig. 4-1 illustrates the buses in an ATE system. The following are some of the buses that an ATE system can use:

1. A peripheral bus, which the controller uses to communicate with the peripherals connected to it. This bus is often the RS-232C, but it may be a manufacturer's own bus, especially if the manufacturer also provides the peripherals (which a number of computer manufacturers nowadays do).

2. An internal set of buses that the controller may use to communicate with certain peripherals and test circuitry built in-house. This bus could be a 16-bit binary bus, as is available on such controllers as the Hewlett-Packard model 26.

3. An internal set of buses that the controller uses to communicate within itself.

4. The IEEE-488 bus to control test equipment. If the devices in the ATE system have only an IEEE-488 bus capability, for example, the controller must have an IEEE-488 capability. If the manufacturer designs and builds the stimuli, measuring instruments, and switching system in the ATE system, any bus may be used if it is compatible with the devices and the controller and serves the designer's purposes. It would be wise to include the IEEE-488 capability unless one were sure that a requirement for it would never exist. It should be mentioned that the requirements for MATE (Modular Automatic Test Equipment) by the U.S. Air Force will also affect instrument control techniques.

Controller Memory   The controller requires enough memory to perform the tests in a timely manner. If the internal memory is inadequate, the controller will be unable to run the test or will have to take the time to use a mass storage device. Controllers generally have a resident memory and may accept plug-in memory boards to expand the memory capability. The amount of memory that the controller requires will depend, of course, on the test programs themselves. The programmer must analyze the tasks that each test program will perform to test the UUTs that the ATE system will support. A factor should be added to allow for future support expansion. The UUT that has the largest memory requirements will determine the final memory requirements of the controller.

The controller must be capable of expanding its memory as test requirements increase. One would be foolhardy to purchase a controller with a

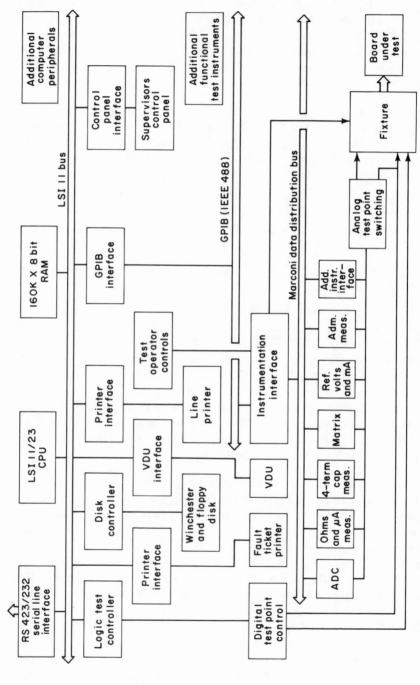

Fig. 4-1 Block diagram of the Marconi System 80 In-circuit Test System showing its buses. See Fig. 4-9 for the LSI-11/23 CPU used here. (*Courtesy of Marconi Instruments.*)

maximum expandable memory capacity of 128K bytes, for example, if the UUT requires 125K bytes. A 3 percent increase in the test program would already exceed the memory capacity. One should also investigate the possibility of using memory-reducing techniques, such as the use of signature analysis and intelligent instruments.

Access to Mass Storage   Each controller must generally access mass storage in some form in order to read in the test program and store programs and data. Common storage media are hard disk, floppy disk, magnetic tape, and cassette. A number of controllers have the mass storage built in, while others have a port with the ability to tie in to a mass storage medium.

The type of mass medium that the controller uses will again depend on the requirements of the test program. Desktop calculators frequently use cassette or floppy disk, while ICTs generally use disk storage because of its high data-storage capabilities. The ICT device library and interactive software for the creation of the test program require a device capable of storing the large number of instructions and amount of data involved. A functional tester dedicated to the testing of one type of UUT may require only a desktop calculator with a cassette built in.

Ease of Programming and Operation   The easier and faster a programmer can produce a test program and an operator can run through a test, the less it will cost to test a UUT. Many ICTs come with a software package that requires minimal programming to create a test program. The capability of creating such a program quickly would weigh heavily in any decision to select a particular controller. With any ATE system, the programming language must allow the user to create and debug a program quickly and with as little programming expertise as possible. The controller should generally have the capability of being programmed in one of the familiar languages, such as BASIC or PASCAL.

Operator-machine Interface   A controller must provide for some communication between the operator and itself. How extensive this capability will have to be depends on many factors. If an ICT will have a complete software package provided with it, the controller may need only an operator's keypad or a few switches. In some instances, a Start Test switch and pass and fail lights will satisfy all requirements.

If the user must program the ATE, a keyboard, CRT, mass storage medium, and a printer may be required. In such a case, the ability of a controller to interface with peripherals (e.g., the inclusion of an RS-232C port) assumes more importance.

Controller Speed   The inherent speed of the controller could assume importance in lengthy tests or when large amounts of data are involved. The use of benchmark programs to compare controllers has caused some controversy and one should use them with care. The use of intelligent instruments and such techniques as signature analysis could also speed up tests somewhat, but these possibilities should be investigated beforehand.

A number of controllers are available on the market today. This chapter will briefly cover examples of desktop calculators, minicomputers, and bus controllers. A later chapter will feature the software of these devices.

HEWLETT-PACKARD SERIES 200 MODEL 26 COMPUTER SYSTEM

The Model 26 follows Hewlett-Packard's 9825 and 9835 computing controllers. (The HP 3060A Board Test System uses the 9825 as its controller).

The Model 26 is shown in Fig. 4-2. A block diagram is shown in Fig. 4-3. The Model 26 is built around the MC68000 16-bit microprocessor, with 32-bit architecture. For operator input, it has a keyboard, numeric keypad, and 10 user-definable special function keys that are useful for editing, cursor control, and system control. The programmer can utilize the keys for special test functions. One key can be set to represent yes, for example, and another to represent no. The operator can then respond to a yes-no question from the controller by pressing one of the two special function keys. The Model 26 has keyboards available in English, French, German, Spanish, Swedish/ Finnish, and Japanese.

The Model 26 has a 178-mm (7-in) CRT display with an alphanumeric capability of 25 lines by 50 characters. The CRT has a full graphics capability with a resolution of 400 dots (horizontal) by 300 dots (vertical). The CRT can display requests, test results, and other information. It allows the pro-

Fig. 4-2 Hewlett-Packard Series 200 Model 26 Computer System. (*Courtesy Hewlett-Packard Company.*)

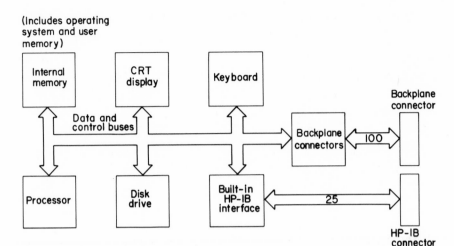

(Includes operating system and user memory)

Internal memory

CRT display

Keyboard

Backplane connector

Data and control buses

Backplane connectors

100

Processor

Disk drive

Built-in HP-IB interface

25

HP-IB connector

Fig. 4-3 Block diagram of the Model 26 Computer System. (*Courtesy of Hewlett-Packard Company.*)

grammer to reduce complex or lengthy test results to a meaningful visual display. One can also graph a series of test results. If the CRT size is inadequate for a particular application, it can be interfaced to another CRT. A Model 36 is also available with a larger CRT.

The Model 26 features a built-in HP-IB (IEEE-488) capability. Optional interface cards allow the user to include other IEEE-488 channels or interface with devices compatible with RS-232C bit serial, GPIO bit parallel, and binary-coded decimal (BCD) formats of data transfer.

An internal read-write memory allows internal memory expansion up to 2 megabytes in 256K-byte increments. A total of 6 megabytes may be used with optional expansion capabilities. A built-in 133-mm (5.25-in) flexible disk provides at least 260K bytes of storage for programs and data.

Hewlett-Packard has three languages available in RAM (through a disk) and ROM: PASCAL, HPL, and HP Enhanced BASIC. HPL is a high-level language that came with the 9825. Users with 9825 programs can enter them into a Model 26 that is configured with HPL capability.

HP Enhanced BASIC has over 200 operators, functions, and statements available in a form that is easy to understand. The following are some software-related features:

1. The use of multicharacter variable names and line labels allows the programmer to write programs that are easier to understand. Other programmers who must interpret the program later will find it easier to determine what the program does. The use of a variable such as "Frequency," for example, is easier to understand than "F" or "Fr." Such a

capability will contribute considerably to software reliability, as will be discussed in a later chapter.

2. Error-trapping allows the programmer to specify a number of actions (provide a beep, display an error message) that will occur in case of an error.

3. Dynamic allocation and deallocation of memory allows more efficient memory management.

4. IF THEN ELSE END IF statement allows block-structured programming. This capability can also contribute to software reliability.

5. A program editor can be called up with a single key. The editor will catch such mistakes as syntaxing errors at program entry.

The Model 26 has 15 levels of programmable software interrupts available. It can thus perform other tasks between the times that devices sent interrupts requesting service.

DATA GENERAL NOVA 4/C COMPUTER

The NOVA 4/C is used as the controller in a number of ATE systems, including the Fairchild 3500 ICT. The NOVA 4/C basically contains a single 38-cm (15-in) CPU board with up to 64K bytes of MOS memory. The board contains a real-time clock, four accumulators, a stack pointer, and a frame pointer. The word length is 16 bits. The memory cycle time is 400 ns.

The CPU board resides in a 14.6-cm (5.75-in) or 26.7-cm (10.5-in) rack mount unit with a virtual console, shown in Fig. 4-4. The 14.6-cm rack mount accommodates up to five boards, which will include the CPU board and four I/O boards. The 26.7-cm rack accommodates the CPU board and up to 15 I/O boards.

The NOVA 4/C is compatible with Data General's peripherals and a number of others on the market. These peripherals include disk drives, magnetic tape units, displays, printers, communication equipment, and data acquisition and control equipment. The NOVA 4/C will handle all NOVA system and application software under Data General's real-time disk operating system (RDOS), real-time operating system (RTOS), and disk operating system (DOS).

TEKTRONIX 4041 COMPUTER/CONTROLLER

The 4041, shown in Fig. 4-5, is a 16-bit instrument controller with both RS-232C and IEEE-488 interfaces. It contains a Motorola 68000 microprocessor, a device used for computational, data-handling, and control functions in a number of ATE controllers. The internal memory capability of the 4041 extends up to 160K bytes.

Fig. 4-4 Data General Nova 4/C Computer installed in a standard cabinet. (*Courtesy of Data General Corporation.*)

The test program generally resides on a magnetic tape cartridge, although one can enter a program through one of the interface ports. The front panel houses a magnetic tape drive for program entry.

The front panel also contains a thermal printer, which gives hard-copy results and system information. A 20-character front panel display provides information and prompts the operator. Eighteen front-panel keys allow the operator to interface with the 4041. The keys perform the following functions:

Auto-Load: This key loads the program from magnetic tape and begins program execution.

Abort: This key halts program operation or passes control to a predefined handler routine.

Pause: This key halts program execution.

Proceed: This key causes the program to resume after a Pause or Abort has been executed. The key also delimits the operator's input when com-

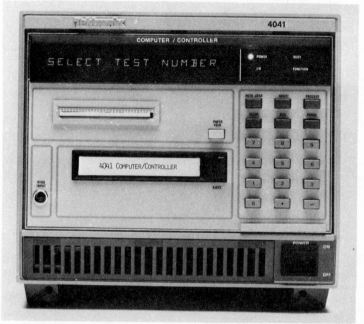

Fig. 4-5 Tektronix 4041 Computer/Controller (*Courtesy of Tektronix, Inc.*)

plying with a program Input statement, which reads in information that the operator enters for use in the program. This entry generally occurs after the program prompts the operator to make the entry by means of the front-panel display.

Clear: This key clears the display.

EEX: This key allows the operator to use scientific notation when entering data. Any numbers the operator enters after pressing EEX become exponents.

Ten numerical keys on the front panel have two uses. First, they allow entry of numerical data when the program requests an entry with the Input statement. Second, they act as user-defined special-function keys. The test program can assign subroutines to each key and the operator can execute them by pressing the appropriate key. Two remaining keys are decimal point and minus. The 18 keys on the front panel and the test program tape cartridge provide primary control.

The 4041 operates as a bus controller in ATE or a test-equipment cluster. It manages the GPIB and controls the devices interfaced to the bus. To accomplish these tasks, the 4041 implements the following IEEE-488 subset capabilities:

SH1, Source Handshake

AH1, Acceptor Handshake

T6, Basic Talker, serial poll, unaddress if my listen address (MLA) is received.

L4, Basic Listener, unaddress if MTA (my talk address) is received.

SR1, Service Request

RL1, Remote-Local

PP1, Parallel Poll: Remote configuration

DC1, Device Clear

DT1, Device Trigger

C1, System Controller

C2, Controller: Send IFC and take charge

C3, Controller: Send REN (Remote Enable)

C4, Controller: Respond to SRQ (Service Request)

C9, Controller: Send IF messages, receive control, pass control, parallel poll, take command synchronously.

The 4041 also features an enhanced BASIC as a programming language. The program development features include an editor, debugging tools, and program and file management. The programmer programs the 4041 by means of an optional keyboard or a terminal interfaced with the RS-232C port. Plotting, graphic, and waveform processing functions are available on ROM packs that plug in to the base of the 4041.

FLUKE 1720A INSTRUMENT CONTROLLER

The CRT of the 1720A is a touch-sensitive display that functions as a programmable "operator keyboard." Fig. 4-6 shows the 1720A with a menu displayed. The operator can press the item desired on the screen and the program will use that selection as though the operator has pressed a panel switch or entered the choice into a keyboard. The touch-sensitive display thus serves as the operator's means of communicating with the controller. As can be seen in Fig. 4-6, the front panel is devoid of any other operator controls.

The advantages of using such a display are obvious. A programmer can set up menus and labels that match the capabilities of the operators involved and the particular requirements of the test. Prompts and highlighted areas

Fig. 4-6 Fluke 1720A Instrument Controller. The programmable touch-sensitive screen provides an operator interface with the controller section. The keyboard provides an interface for programming. (*Courtesy of John Fluke Mfg. Co., Inc.*)

will draw attention to areas of importance and speed up the tests. The programmer can combine characters and graphics to achieve an operator interface that fits each situation.

The 12.7 by 22.9 cm (5 by 9 in) CRT display itself provides 16 lines of 80 characters each, or 8 lines of 40 double-size characters. It contains 1280 bytes of refresh memory to handle the 16 by 80 character capability of the screen. Its video capabilities include reverse video, blinking, underline, and highlighting.

A switch matrix that passes 66 percent of the light overlays the CRT display. The layout of the matrix is shown in Fig. 4-7. Sixty switch areas connect to the interface circuitry and allow the programmer to set up soft keys anywhere within the 6 by 10 matrix.

The touch-sensitive display consists of two polyester sheets, each of which is coated on one side with an ultrathin layer of sectional gold. Each section corresponds to a switch position in the matrix. The sections have hairlines etched through them that dissect them and create an open circuit, as shown in Fig. 4-8. The gold conducting surfaces of the sections on each sheet sit at right angles to those on the other sheet. The sheets are separated by a few millimeters.

When the switch is pressed, the two sections make contact and complete the circuit. One section serves as the "row" switch and the other as the "column" switch. When the operator presses a particular switch, the interface circuitry will detect the particular row and column where the circuit has been completed. The switch circuitry passes this information to the controller, where it is provided to the test program.

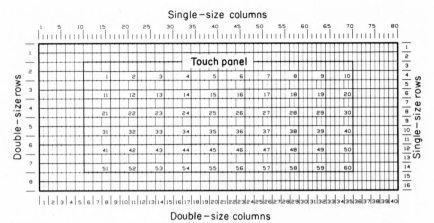

Fig. 4-7 Matrix layout for the 1720A touch-sensitive display. One can program any of the switch areas with prompts or messages. (*Courtesy of John Fluke Mfg. Co., Inc.*)

The 1720A features a single-head, double-density floppy disk with 200 bytes of mass storage. The 133-mm (5.25-in) diskette that is used is soft-sectored. The data is organized into 400 blocks of 512 bytes each, divided over 40 tracks. An optional 128K- or 256K-byte E Disk (electronic disk) and up to 512 bytes of bubble memory is also available.

The 1720A also contains 60K bytes of resident memory, of which 24K bytes are available to the user when the standard BASIC interpreter is in

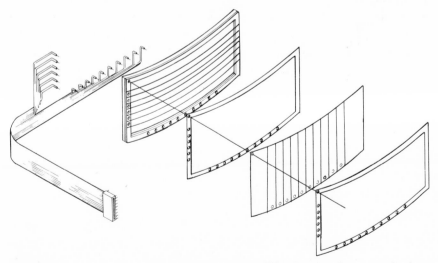

Fig. 4-8 Layout of the touch-sensitive lay of the 1720A showing the row and column connections. (*Courtesy of John Fluke Mfg. Co., Inc.*)

use. Dual IEEE-488 and dual RS-232C interfaces are also available. The 1720A also contains a real-time 4-year calendar clock, which gives day, month, year, and hours, minutes, and milliseconds per day. A battery provides a 2-month backup.

A keyboard plugs into the 1720A to provide an interface for programming. The controller uses an enhanced BASIC as its language. Options include FORTRAN, PASCAL, and assembly language.

Fig. 4-9 The LSI-11/23 microcomputer used in ATE systems consists of two 13.2-cm (5.2-in) by 22.6-cm (8.9-in) boards and backplane. (*Courtesy of Digital Equipment Corporation.*)

REFERENCES

Anundson, Robert L.: "2nd-Generation GPIB Equipment Offers Easy-to-Use Improvements," *EDN*, Aug. 19, 1981, pp. 165–172.

Runyon, Stan: "Compatible-Instrument Clusters Promise Speedier, Smarter Bench Measurements," *Electronic Design*, Oct. 11, 1979, pp. 85–89.

5

ATE SOFTWARE

Before an organization can place a manual test set into operation, an engineer must write a test procedure from the test-requirements specification. The procedure describes the steps that the technician must take to test the UUT. The procedure may give the switch positions, connections, test-equipment settings, measurements, and tolerances. If the technician follows the entire procedure, the UUT will supposedly be thoroughly tested.

THE ATE PROGRAM

The equivalent of the written step-by-step procedure in ATE, of course, is the test program. Since the controller is basically a computer, those familiar with computer programming will recognize many instructions from other applications. An engineer who uses a Model 26 desktop computer as the controller for an in-house ATE system, for example, will use the same instructions for programming as the engineer who uses the Model 26 to design circuits. Both engineers would use such common instructions as those that perform arithmetic and logical operations, loops, jumps, arrays, and print and display functions. As a result, programming for ATE generally requires the same expertise and experience as any other program. The ATE program, however, has two differences.

1. The complex blend of hardware and software in ATE requires that a programmer have a working knowledge of both UUT and ATE hardware and its idiosyncracies (just as the ATE hardware engineer should know the ATE and UUT software). In many organizations, the ATE engineer handles both hardware and software.

2. Since the ATE controller interfaces with buses that tie into other devices,

the programmer must become familiar with the special bus instructions and their idiosyncracies. The controller communicates with other instruments on the bus with these instructions and will probably have to use different codes and formats for each of the devices on the bus.

GPIB SOFTWARE DIFFICULTIES

Adequate information concerning the device requirements may be difficult to obtain. The IEEE-488 standard covers the functional, electrical, and mechanical aspects of the GPIB, but it allows instrument manufacturers the freedom to select the operational requirements of their instruments.

With one manufacturer's DMM, for example, the controller must send the string "F1" to set it up for dc volts, while another DMM requires a "Y" as part of its setup string. One manufacturer of function generators requires that the controller send commands only for those functions that must be changed from the last setup. Other manufacturers require that the message cover every setup parameter, whether or not it has already been set up.

As a result, the programmer must gather sufficient operational detail on each device on the bus, and on the bus itself, to assure the proper response to commands and data. Such information resides in the manuals of the controller and device manufacturers, but sometimes the information provided is unclear or misleading or is left out altogether. With a number of devices on the bus, the programmer may have to spend weeks at the beginning of a project just gathering information and getting clarifications.

Some ATE manufacturers provide programming stations to facilitate the creation of test programs for their ATE systems without interfering with test operations. Such stations often contain a keyboard and CRT for creating the program, a disk to provide storage, and a printer for a hard copy. The station often has an interface that allows it to tie into the ATE system for online programming functions. Fig. 5-1 shows a programming station.

ATE SOFTWARE PACKAGES

A number of ATE manufacturers provide device libraries of test subroutines or device characteristics, as well as software packages for test-program preparation. Such software interacts with the programmer during the preparation of a dedicated test program. It should be pointed out that manufacturers often provide software packages that preclude the need for a programmer. A test engineer may serve as a more expert "programmer" in these instances because of familiarity with test and diagnostic techniques. The "programming" of many ATE systems available today consists of providing circuit data and some testing and diagnostic information based on a simple format.

The GenRad 1796 Digital/Analog Test System, for example, comes with

Fig. 5-1 Fluke 3051B Programming Station with terminal, keyboard, and dual, double-sided floppy disk drive. (*Courtesy of Fluke Automated Systems.*)

CAPS, its own software package. As a beginning step in the production of a test program, a clerical worker can type in the required data on the device, pins, and connections of the circuit board to be tested on the data terminal of the 1796.

Hewlett-Packard 3060A Software

The 3060A Board Test System is another example of an ATE system that comes with an extensive software package. The 3060A faces two separate testing problems, as do many ATE systems: the static testing of such combinational devices as gates, and the dynamic testing of others, such as microprocessors.

The 3060A In-Circuit Program Generator (IPG) also allows an operator without technical training and but a few hours of instruction to enter circuit data into the 9825A Computing Controller of the system. IPG then automatically creates a complete in-circuit test program for the components on the board. It specifies the in-circuit measurement tools, selects the guard points, and produces the test fixture wiring layout.

Fig. 5-2 illustrates the entry of data into the 3060A for the static test of a two-input, four-output decoder. The enable, inputs, and outputs of the

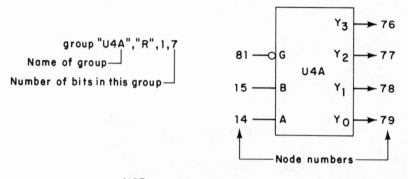

group "U4A","R",1,7
Name of group ⌐
Number of bits in this group ⌐

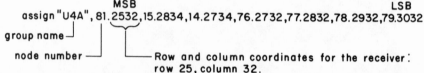

MSB   LSB
assign "U4A", 81.2532,15.2834,14.2734,76.2732,77.2832,78.2932,79.3032
group name ⌐
node number ⌐   ⌐ Row and column coordinates for the receiver:
row 25, column 32.

Fig. 5-2 Example of HP3060A data entry for a two-input (pins A and B), four-output (Y_0-Y_3) decoder. (Pin G is an enable.) The **group** statement allocates memory space and the **assign** statement allots seven receivers to check the inputs and outputs. (*Courtesy of Hewlett-Packard Company.*)

decoder total seven pins. The group statement allocates the memory space for the information that the controller will store for the group of seven decoder pins.

The assign statement allots seven receivers to the group to allow the test system to check inputs and outputs. The statement matches node numbers of the board to the row and column coordinates of the corresponding receiver. The statement lists the enable first, followed by the inputs and outputs, in that order. A similar procedure will program the drivers that will input the test patterns at the board. The apply statement initiates test patterns that are output to the drivers. When the program is run, the drivers will stimulate the board inputs with the test patterns while the receivers measure the board responses. The main program will call verification subroutines from the device library for each of the devices as it is tested. The receive statement assigns receiver data to a variable that the program passes to the subroutines to verify that the device nodes provide the correct response. An incorrect response causes the subroutine to set a flag, which the main program will detect, causing it to print out an error message.

To program the 3060A in this manner, then, the operator can follow a few simple instructions and enter the data using the statements (receive, apply, etc.) given in the required format. The program generator will bring all of the information together as required to produce a final test program for the board.

GPIB INSTRUCTIONS

The ATE controller requires a number of software instructions that allow it to use the GPIB. The instructions generally allow the controller to accomplish the following:

1. Send commands and data over the bus to the devices that are interfaced to the bus.

2. Read in data and status from the devices on the bus.

3. Perform bus management tasks.

Fig. 5-3 contains some example instructions in HPL (Hewlett-Packard Language) for the 9825A desktop calculator. Note that the number 7 appears after some instructions, either by itself or as the first digit of a three-digit code (trg 711). As shown in Fig. 5-4, the 7 represents the HP-IB select code. An action that affects all of the devices interfaced to the bus would require that the controller send only a 7, as with trg 7.

The three-digit code that follows some instructions represents the address of a device on the bus. A device-dependent action would require the specific address of the device involved. An instruction such as wrt 711 addresses the device on bus 7 whose address switches are set for an address of 11.

The 9825A can use the wrt instruction to send operational messages to the devices on the bus. These messages would include instructions that set up measuring instruments to make measurements (e.g., set a counter to the time interval mode) or a stimulus to provide a signal (e.g., set up a frequency synthesizer to output a sine wave). The instruction wrt 705, "YVL" would set up a Systron-Donner 7344A DMM to measure dc volts (The "Y" portion of the string sets this) on the Auto Range ("V") and in the Sample Mode ("L"). The wrt command addresses the DMM as a listener, then sends the string YVL one byte at a time over the GPIB data bus (terminated with a carriage return and line feed.) When the DMM receives the string, its GPIB circuits switch the DMM to dc volts, Auto Range, and Sample Mode.

Fig. 5-5 lists the IEEE-488 operational control characters for the 7344A. The programmer can utilize these characters with the wrt command to achieve the DMM setups required.

The 9825A dev instruction allows one to substitute a meaningful label for the address. The equ instruction allows the same to be done with the bus message. The following statements at the beginning of a program would make such a substitution throughout the rest of the program:

```
dev 710,"DVM"
equ"DC VOLTS","YVL"
```

Message name	Description	Sample operations
Data	Output text and variables to single devices.	wrt 701, "total = ",A wrt"Printer",A,B,C
	Output single characters.	wtb 701,H
	Input data from a device.	red 711,A$,B$
	Input single characters.	rdb(711)→A
	Specify device address and send data in the form of ASCII characters.	cmd 7,"?U-","L10" cmd"dvm","L10"
	Output data to multiple listeners.	wrt"dvm,printer","L10" cmd"?UK","L10"
	Transfer data from device to device.	cmd"?K"
Trigger	Send a Group Execute Trigger to all instruments.	trg 7
	Send a GET to selected devices.	trg 711
Clear	Clear all devices.	clr 7
	Clear selected devices.	clr 711
Remote	Enable remote mode on all devices. Switching the calculator on also sends a Remote message.	rem 7
	Set remote mode on selected device.	rem 711
Local	Return selected device to local mode.	lcl 722
Local lockout	Prevent all devices from returning to local mode.	llo 7
Clear lockout/ Set local	Set local mode and disable local lockout on all devices. Reset also sends this message.	lcl 7
Pass Control	Transfer bus control to a selected device.	pct 723
Require Service Status Byte	Request Service from the controller and send an 8-bit status byte for response to a Serial Poll.	rqs 7,105
Status Bit	Bit and logic level for responses to a Parallel Poll.	rqs 7,64
Abort	Clear all bus operations and return control to the original controller. Reset also sends an abort message.	cli 7

Fig. 5-3 Sample HP-IB operations with the HP9825A desktop computer. Note the similarity between some commands and the basic GPIB functions. (*Courtesy of Hewlett-Packard Company.*)

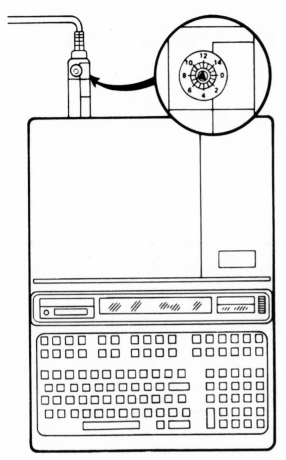

Fig. 5-4 Interface addressing on a desktop computer. The address select switch in this example is set to a 7. I/O instructions must use address 7 to address this port. (*Courtesy of Hewlett-Packard Company.*)

Afterward, the programmer could set up the DMM for dc volts each time as follows:

wrt "DVM","DC VOLTS"

A primary instruction for reading data from the bus with the 9825A is the red instruction. (The wrt instruction would probably precede red at some point in the program in order to set up the device that will provide the data.) The statement red 706,A would address device 706 as a talker, command it to send the data over the data bus, then read in the value and assign it to the variable A. From that point on, the program would use the variable A just as it would if it had assigned the measured value to it in the program.

| Control | ASCII characters | Data input-output code | | | | | | |
		Bit 7	Bit 6	Bit 5	Bit 4	Bit 3	Bit 2	Bit 1
Function								
VDC	Y	1	0	1	1	0	0	1
VAC	Z	1	0	1	1	0	1	0
kΩ	[	1	0	1	1	0	1	1
Range								
Auto	V	1	0	1	0	1	1	0
0.2	U	1	0	1	0	1	0	1
2	T	1	0	1	0	1	0	0
20	S	1	0	1	0	0	1	1
200	R	1	0	1	0	0	1	0
2000	Q	1	0	1	0	0	0	1
20000	P	1	0	1	0	0	0	0
Hold	D	1	0	0	0	1	0	0
Sample	L	1	0	0	1	1	0	0
Read	C	1	0	0	0	1	1	1

Fig. 5-5 IEEE-488 program control characters for the Systron Donner 7344A DMM. One must program the controller to send a combination of characters over the GPIB to set up the 7344A for the particular measurement desired. (*Courtesy of Systron Donner.*)

One must be careful of the format of bus commands. The format commands assign various portions of the input string to particular variables. This separates the numerical value of the measurement from other information that the talker might send. If the device sends a message terminator, for example, a format command can separate the terminator from the rest of the message. If status information precedes the numerical data, a format statement can separate them. Consider the following simple routine for a 7344A measurement:

```
dev 710, "DVM"
fmt 9,c5,e9
red "DVM.9",A$[1], V
```

Format statement 9 declares that the first five characters from the bus will be placed in dummy string variable A$[1] in the red statement. The remaining nine characters will be assigned to the variable V. The message

ASCII print out														Readout 6344A	
	V	D	C	+	1	9	8	7	6	E		2		+ 198.76 VDC	200 Range
O	L	V	D	C	+	0	0	0	0	0	E		3	+ 00.000 VDC	(20) Range
		V	A	C		1	9	8	7	6	E		2	198.76 VAC	200 Range
			k	Ω		1	9	8	5	5	E		3	198.55 kΩ	200 Range
1	2	3	4	5	6	7	8	9	10	11	12	13	14	Bytes	

Note: Byte 15,CR and 16,LI, are not printed out.

Fig. 5-6 Examples of IEEE-488 output formats for the 7344A DMM. The left column gives the ASCII equivalent of the setup parameters in the right column. (*Courtesy of Systron Donner.*)

from the 7344A contains a string of five characters that provide status information, then nine characters that contain the numerical value of the measurement. The statement red "DVM.9" reads the value from the DMM and arranges it according to format 9. Fig. 5-6 shows the IEEE-488 output format for the 7344A.

The remaining instructions and sample operations in Fig. 5-3 should be studied to gain familiarity with bus commands. The 9825A is capable of sending such GPIB commands as Group Execute Trigger (instruction trg), Device Clear (clr), Remote (rem), Local (lcl), and others that initiate the basic GPIB functions covered in Chap. 2.

MODEL 26 ENHANCED BASIC

It may be instructive to compare some statements of the Enhanced BASIC of Hewlett-Packard's Model 26 desktop computer with the HPL of the 9825A. The equivalent of the 9825A dev statement is the ASSIGN statement. It follows the format ASSIGN (I/O path name) TO (device selector code). For example,

ASSIGN @ Ckt TO 2
ASSIGN @ Dmm TO 705

The latter statement assigns @ Dmm as an equivalent to device 705. Throughout the remainder of the program, the programmer can substitute @ Ckt for device 2 and @ Dmm for device 705.

The equivalent of the wrt statement for the 9826A is the OUTPUT statement. This statement takes the form OUTPUT (Destination); (Expressions). For example,

OUTPUT @ Device; Data$

This statement outputs the value in variable Data$ to the device specified by @Device to a particular device selector, as covered above. The expressions can be any valid numeric or string expression.

The equivalent of the red statement is the ENTER statement. It takes the form ENTER (Source); (Variables). For example,

ENTER @Meter; Volts

This instruction will input data from the device designated by @Meter and assign the value of the input data to the variable Volts.

The following are examples of other I/O instructions available with Hewlett-Packard's Enhanced BASIC, along with their description of each one. As with the 9825A instructions, one should note the similarity between Model 26 instructions and the bus commands covered in Chap. 2.

CMD: Used with the SEND statement to send numeric or string expressions over the HP-IB with ATN true.

DATA: Used with the SEND statement to send numeric or string expressions over the HP-IB with ATN false if the computer is the active controller and is addressed to talk.

ENABLE INTR: Enables the specified interface to generate an interrupt which can cause end-of-statement branches.

LOCAL: Returns all specified devices to their local state.

LOCAL LOCKOUT: Sends the LLO (local lockout) message, preventing an operator from returning the device to local control by its front panel.

PPOLL CONFIGURE: Programs the logical sense and data bus line on which the specified device responds to a parallel poll.

PPOLL UNCONFIGURE: Disables the parallel poll response of the specified devices.

REMOTE: Places HP-IB devices having remote/local capabilities into the remote state of operation.

SEND: Sends control information and data to an HP-IB interface.

TALK: Used with SEND command to define which devices talk on GPIB.

TRIGGER: Initiates device-dependent action from either a selected device or all devices addressed to listen on the HP-IB.

TEKTRONIX 4041 INSTRUMENT CONTROLLER

The 4041 also uses an enhanced BASIC similar to that used in other types of applications. The differences, of course, lie in the special GPIB commands. The following is a list of some of them with a description of each one. Again, one should note the similarity between the following commands and the GPIB commands of the same or similar name.

ATN: Sends universal and addressed commands from the controller and designates peripherals as talkers and listeners for data transfer.

DCL: Device Clear. Returns all devices on the bus to their device-dependent quiescent state.

EOI: Indicates the end of a data transfer sequence from a talker.

GET: Remotely operates a device connected to the GPIB.

GTL: Allows a device to accept input and instruction from its front panel controls only.

IFC: Interface Clear. Places all devices on the bus in a device-dependent state, and takes controller-in-charge status from another controller on the bus.

POLL: Executes a serial poll on the GPIB.

PPC: Configures the bus for a parallel poll

PPU: Unconfigures the bus from a parallel poll.

REN: Invoked by the system controller. Allows the controller-in-charge to operate devices on the bus remotely.

SDC: Clears all specified devices by their listen addresses.

SPD: Returns all devices from their serial poll enable state.

SPE: Causes each device on the bus to respond with its status message when addressed to talk.

SRQ: Requests service from the controller, if the 4041 operates on a bus with another controller in charge.

TCT: Passes controller-in-charge status to another device on the bus.

As with the other controllers, such instructions as ATN (Attention), GTL (Go To Local), IFC (Interface Clear), REN (Remote Enable), SPE (Serial Poll Enable), and the others were all covered in Chap. 2.

PROGRAMMING POWER SUPPLIES

Chap. 3 discussed the Kepco BOP power supply, which allows control of both voltage and current and features an automatic crossover between constant voltage and constant current modes. To program the output voltage or current remotely, one can vary the voltage at the programming input terminals.

Fig. 5-7 shows the block diagram for the Kepco SNR 488 programmer, which converts a GPIB message to a voltage output that controls the power supply output. The SNR 488 can take up to eight programming cards to control up to eight power supplies.

The SNR 488 receives its commands from the controller over the GPIB. The controller sends an address byte, followed by nine data bytes. The ATN line goes true with the first byte, which the SNR 488 will interpret as an address. If that address corresponds to the address set in at the address switches, the SNR 488 will respond to the data messages that follow. The SNR 488 will then convert the input ASCII data to hexadecimal format and pass it on to the internal bus.

Three bits of the first byte contain the address of the individual card. If the input address corresponds to those set at the internal card address select switch, that card of the SNR 488 will respond and enable the control logic. All unaddressed cards will remain disabled.

The next character will be a "=" that prompts the control circuits to enable the transfer of the next seven bytes of data. Shift commands bring the seven data bytes into a shift register. After the last byte, a control signal strobes the parallel data into a set of latches. The latches provide inputs to two digital-to-analog converters (DACs). The user can connect up the DAC outputs to provide whatever control is desired. One DAC can set the power supply output voltage and the other can set the current limit.

The programming of the BOP power supply differs from the programming of other types of test equipment in that one programs the *proportion* of full-scale output that is desired rather than the desired output itself. Suppose one wants to program a 36-V, 10-A power supply for a 20-V output with a 6-A current limit. The following formula will compute the proportional output voltage for programming purposes:

$$E_P = \frac{999}{E_{fs}} \times E_d$$

where E_P = proportional output voltage (The actual value that will be sent over the GPIB.)

E_d = desired output voltage

E_{fs} = full-scale output voltage (This is 36 V in this example.)

Substituting a full-scale output of 36 V and a desired output of 20 V will give a value for programming of 555.

The following formula will provide the proportional output current:

$$I_p = \frac{999}{I_{fs}} \times I_d$$

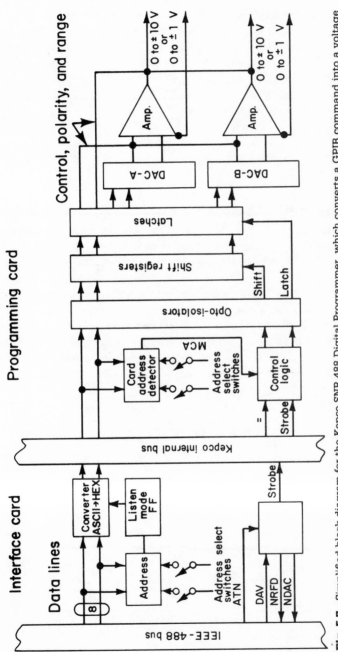

Fig. 5-7 Simplified block diagram for the Kepco SNR 488 Digital Programmer, which converts a GPIB command into a voltage that controls a power supply output. (*Courtesy of Kepco, Inc.*)

Substituting a full scale output of 10 A in the denominator and a desired current limit of 6 A in the numerator will give a value of 599.

The programming now is quite simple. The pertinent values are arranged in the following order: (GPIB address)(=)(C)(voltage)(current). The C in the format is a control character that sets the output range and polarity. As stated, the symbol " = " enables the transfer of data. For the example, one would program the controller to send the following message over the bus to the power supply set to address 2.

2 = 0 555 599

The control character 0 sets a positive output at the high range.

SWITCHING SYSTEM REQUIREMENTS

The test program contains the commands that the controller sends to the switching system to connect devices to each other or to UUT test points. Fig. 5-8 shows typical connections to a switching system for an in-house ATE system that was built to test a particular subassembly. UUT connector pin 38 connects through the test cable to pin 17 on the test connector, which is in turn connected to scanner pin 1. To measure the frequency at UUT pin 38, the test program must connect scanner input pin 1 to output pin 2. (The inconsistency of pin numbers, i.e., pin 17 to pin 38 to pin 1, is given here as a realistic example in order to demonstrate the confusion a programmer can face when setting up an ATE switching system. The errors

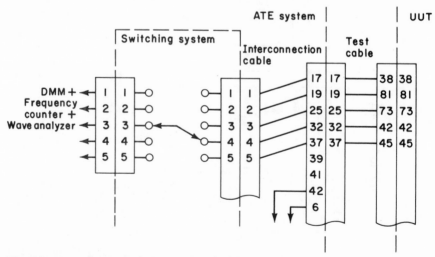

Fig. 5-8 Example of connections between the UUT and the test panel, scanner, and test equipment of an ATE system.

that arise will be covered in a later chapter on software reliability.) The programmer would thus have to know that UUT pin 38 connects through the ATE system to scanner input 1 and that the frequency counter connects to output pin 2. The programmer would have to obtain this information from the ATE hardware engineer.

The hardware engineer could provide a list that is similar to the following:

Scanner Connections

Scanner output	Device
Pin 1	DMM
Pin 2	Frequency counter
Pin 3	Wave analyzer
Pin 4	Spare

Scanner input	UUT pin
Pin 1	38
Pin 2	81
Pin 3	73
Pin 4	42
Pin 5	45
.	.
.	.
.	.

With perhaps hundreds of pins being connected in a switching system, the possibility is great that a few of them are in error. This will also be covered in a later chapter.

To make the program more understandable later, the programmer can exchange the UUT pin numbers and scanner pin numbers as shown in the following routine:

```
110 "TEST CONNECTOR-SCANNER TABLE": dim S [99]
111 "SCANNER CHANNEL→S [UUT PIN #]":
112    1→S [38]; 2→S [81]; 3→S [73]; 4→S [42]; 5→S [45]
```

Line 110 dimensions array variable S for up to 99 UUT pins. Line 111 gives instructions on interchanging of scanner input and UUT pin numbers in the program. (Any HPL statement in quotation marks and followed by a colon is a nonexecutable software comment.) Line 112 interchanges input pin 1 with UUT pin 38, to which it has been wired; input pin 2 with UUT pin 81, and so forth. The programmer could thus use the term S [38] when sending the scanner command for UUT pin 38. The program will substitute a 1 and activate input channel 1.

The Autex FX30 has two channels, A and B, each of which contain 100 signal paths. The FX30 is described in more detail in Chap. 3.

Fig. 5-9 shows the format for the GPIB message to set up the FX30. The command required to connect UUT pin 38 in the example above would therefore be:

wrt "SCAN", "SA201000ST"

The first two characters, SA, indicate the connection is to channel A. The next three numbers indicate that the scanner is to connect output pin 2 to input pin 1. If the programmer has used the routine above that interchanges scanner pin and UUT pin number, a more meaningful statement would be as follows:

fmt fz2.0;wrt"SCAN","SA2",S[38],"000ST"

The format statement fmt fz2.0 indicates that the variable S [38] will consist of two digits without a decimal place. The rest of the statement accomplishes the same connection as the one above. The controller will substitute the number 01 for S [38] in the command and send the same string as the one above.

ATLAS LANGUAGE

A number of ATE systems use ATLAS (Abbreviated Test Language for All Systems), a UUT test-oriented language. Its popularity is based on its ease of human interpretation. An introduction to the language may be useful to those involved with ATE, even though their present ATE uses another language. Details can vary considerably among ATLAS compilers.

A typical ATLAS statement might consist of three major parts:

1. Action: An Atlas verb specifies the desired action. Examples of stimulus action verbs are APPLY and SETUP. An example of a sensor action verb is MEASURE. A programmer can combine an action verb with a modifier to expand the meaning.

   MEASURE (FREQ)
   READ (FREQ INTO 'FOUT')
   VERIFY (POWER ERRLMT + − 1 DBM)

2. Signal Description: This portion consists of the following:
   a. A noun (e.g., DC SIGNAL) that specifies the signal type.

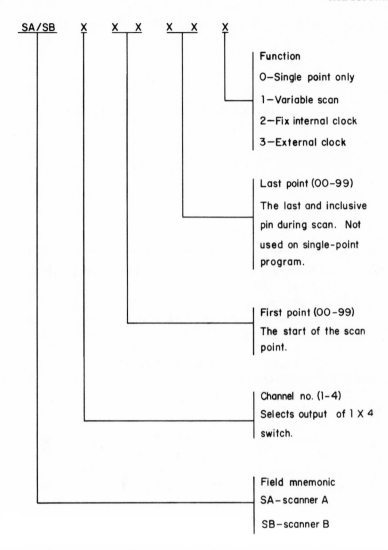

ST = Mnemonic code to start the scan.

Fig. 5-9 GPIB message format to set up the Autek FX30 Coaxial Scanner. The mneumonic ST transmitted after the setup will initiate the scan. (*Courtesy of Autek Systems Corp., Santa Clara, Calif.*)

    b. A statement characteristic, which specifies the required signal values and characteristics. It begins with a modifier mneumonic (e.g., VOLTAGE) followed by a value or range (e.g., 10V; VOLTAGE RANGE 1 V to 1.5 V) and an optional accuracy specification (e.g., ERRLMT + − .1V)

3. UUT Input or Output Connections: The ATLAS instruction CNX speci-fies the UUT connections for high and low inputs or outputs. One form is:

CNX HI J4-1 LO J3$

This statement specifies that the high connection will be at UUT con-nector J4, pin 1 and the low will be at J3.

A stimulus statement that would apply 10 ± 0.01 V dc between UUT pins J2-2 (high) and J1 would follow the format:

APPLY, DC SIGNAL,
VOLTAGE 10V ERRLMT + − .01V
CNX HI J2-2 LO J1 $

The APPLY verb specifies the action. DC SIGNAL, VOLTAGE 10V ERRLMT + − .01 V gives the signal description. CNX HI J2-2 LO J1 $ specifies the UUT connections.

An ATLAS measurement statement closely follows the signal application format. The following is an example:

MEASURE (FREQ ERRLMT + − .02MHZ), AC SIGNAL
   FREQ RANGE 4 MHZ TO 6 MHZ,
      VOLTAGE RANGE 1 V TO 1.5 V,
         CNX HI J1-1 LO J1-2 $

MEASURE FREQ specifies the action, which is to measure the frequency. The associated measurement characteristic (ERRLMT + − .02 MHZ) speci-fied the required measurement accuracy that the program will check for. AC SIGNAL is the noun that specifes the signal type. The statement char-acteristic for the noun covers the next two lines and specifies the signal characteristics and values. The final line specifies the connections. The AT-LAS statement thus specifies a measurement of frequency with an accuracy of ± 0.02 MHz. The counter will measure an ac signal with a signal level of 1 to 1.5 V and a frequency of 4 to 6 MHz. The measurement will be made between UUT pins J1-1 and J1-2.

This brief discussion is intended only to compare one form of ATLAS with other languages. A number of instructions and formats would have to be covered to familiarize oneself completely with ATLAS.

Fig. 5-10, 5-11, and 5-12 show the Bendix ATLAS Composing Terminal (ACT). It translates test requirements into test requirements documents and test programs. The operator has only to enter scratch pad test data and ACT will work with that data to produce the required outputs, including the following:

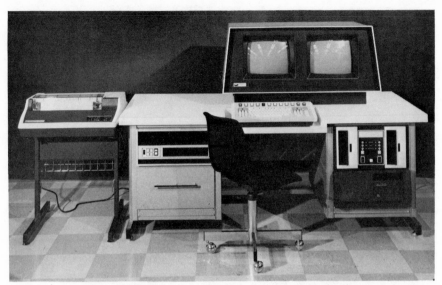

Fig. 5-10 Bendix ATLAS Composing Terminal (ACT) which facilitates creation of test requirement documents and ATLAS test programs. (*Courtesy of Bendix Test Systems Division, Teterboro, N.J.*)

1. An ATLAS test program.
2. Test requirement document in MIL-STD-1519 format. Fig. 5-11 shows the screen of the ACT with a completed ATLAS test program displayed on it.

Fig. 5-11 The ACT display during creation of test requirement data. (*Courtesy of Bendix Test Systems Division, Teterboro, N.J.*)

Fig. 5-12 ACT display showing an ATLAS test program. (*Courtesy of Bendix Test Systems Division, Teterboro, N.J.*)

REFERENCES

ATLAS Language Programming Manual, Hewlett-Packard Company/Automatic Measurement Division, Mar. 15, 1976, pp. 1-1–1-8.

Dynamic Digital Board Testing, Application Note 308-1, Hewlett-Packard Co., Nov. 1980, pp. 4-15.

Humphrey, John R., and Kanram Firooz: "ATE Brings Speedy, Complete Testing via Signature Analysis to LSI-Board Production," *Electronic Design*, Feb. 1, 1980, pp. 75–79.

Jackson, Trudi, and Paul Vais: "Test LSI Boards Functionally on an In-Circuit Tester," *Electronic Design*, Oct. 29, 1981, pp. 137–144.

Jessen, Ken: "In-Circuit Tester Answers μP-Board Challenge," *Electronic Design*, Nov. 8, 1980, pp. 97–101.

Laengrich, Norbert: "Instrument Intelligence Determines 488 Bus Speed," *Electronic Design*, Oct. 15, 1981, pp. 181–185.

Levin, Harold: "Enhanced Simulator Takes On Bus-Structured Logic," *Electronic Design*, Oct. 29, 1981, pp. 153–157.

Liguori, F.: *Automatic Test Equipment: Hardware, Software, and Management*, IEEE Press, New York, 1974, pp. 107–200.

Lippman, Michael D.: "Efficient and Effective μC Testing Requires Careful Preplanning," *EDN*, Feb. 20, 1979, pp. 97–107.

McLeod, Jonah: "ATE Swings Toward Merged In-Circuit, Functional Tests," *Electronic Design*, Oct. 29, 1981, pp. 90–104.

Runyon, Stan: "BASIC Underlies the Multiple Language of Smart Instruments," *Electronic Design*, Oct. 11, 1979, pp. 95–98.

————: "Compatible-Instrument Clusters Promise Speedier, Smarter Bench Measurements," *Electronic Design*, Oct. 11, 1979, pp. 85–89.

Static Digital Testing, Application Note 309-1, Hewlett-Packard Co., Feb. 1981, pp. 2–14.

Stover, Allan C.: "Software Simulation Techniques Improve ATE Quality," *Proceedings ATE Seminar/Exhibit*, June 1982, pp. IV-17–IV-28.

Tilden, Mark, and Bob Ramirez: "GPIB Software Configuration Determines System Performance," *EDN*, Aug. 4, 1982, pp. 137–142.

Young, Will: "An Automated Approach to Generating Test Programs," *Electronics Test*, Oct. 1981, pp. 30–36.

6

ATE PROGRAMS

ATE programs for the testing and troubleshooting of UUTs are generally created in one of two ways:

1. A programmer utilizes a programming language (BASIC, HPL, ATLAS, assembly language, etc.) to write the program.

2. A test engineer, assisted by a typist and possibly a technician, utilizes the test program preparation package supplied with the ATE to create the program.

The creation of a test or diagnostic program using a programming language such as HPL or BASIC follows much the same procedure as the writing of any other program. The only differences may be in the commands that deal with external control of devices and circuitry in the ATE. While other programs may use such external devices as displays, keyboards, and printers to communicate with the operator, the ATE program controls additional devices that make measurements, provide stimuli, switch connections, etc.

Consider the following HPL routine that reads in a measured value from a frequency counter, applies corrections, then sends the corrected value out to a signal generator:

```
45 "SETFRQ":
46 wrt "FCTR", "FREQ"
47 red "FCTR",F
48 if F=)99 and F=(101;gto"PASSF"
49 200-F→F
50 wrt "GEN", "L",F"="
51 gto +2
```

52 "PASSF": wrt 16, "FREQ IN SPEC"

.

.

.

The statement in line 46 sets up the frequency counter to measure frequency. At some previous point in the program, a dev statement was used to substitute "FCTR" for the counter's address. An equ allowed the programmer to use "FREQ" for the setup string in line 46. Line 47 reads in the frequency value. Line 49 subtracts F from 200 and assigns the result to F. This is somewhat equivalent to F = 200 − F in other languages.

The two lines are thus used for external operations in that they set up the counter, then take a reading. Note that the wrt command could be used for non-GPIB devices. In line 52, the wrt statement sends a message to the printer. The red statement might be less common in non-ATE programs, but it can still be used for other operations.

It may be instructive to cover the rest of the routine. Lines 48 and 49 are logical and mathematical operations respectively, and one could find them in other types of programs. Line 50 sends the corrected value to the signal generator if the frequency is out of specification. The character "L" is an operator that the generator recognizes will precede frequency. F, of course, is the computed frequency. The " = " operator specifies that the frequency is in hertz.

MEASUREMENTS

Before a measuring device can measure, the programmer must first set up such parameters as range and function. The controller must then read in the measured value from the bus and use that value in its calculations. In some cases, the controller may have to send a triggering command before it can read in the measurement. An example would be an intelligent instrument that will make a series of measurements, then send the result of a calculation over the bus rather than a measurement itself.

The following routine is a simple one that illustrates the steps that a programmer must go through to read a 28-V 400-Hz ac signal with a Systron-Donner 7344 DMM:

```
33 wrt 705, "ZSL"
34 fmt 9,c5,e9;red 705.9,A$[1],V
35 if V<26 or V>30;gto + 2
36 prt "400Hz PASS";gto + 2
37 prt "400Hz FAIL"
```

.

.

.

Similar routines have been discussed in a previous chapter. Line 33 sets up the 7344A for ac volts. (See the bus control requirements for the 7344A in Chap. 5.) Line 34 formats the input value, then reads it from the GPIB. The address of the 7344A is 705, so line 33 and 34 both use the address rather than a device name. The programmer made this choice because the program makes only one DMM measurement; the use of a device name instead of a device address was felt to be unnecessary.

Line 35 is standard in most measurement programs. It checks the measured value to assure that it lies within allowable limits. In case of failure, the program goes to a routine that prints out a fail indication. Otherwise, it prints out pass and continues on. A potential for error exists in this section, since the programmer could set an invalid condition that would indicate a pass even when the UUT fails. This situation will be covered in a later section on ATE software reliability.

COMPARISON OF MEASUREMENT PROGRAMS

It may be instructive at this point to compare the programs of a few computers in order to gain an insight into their similarities and differences. Many computers can be used as ATE controllers, so it would be impractical to compare them all. The following programs all accomplish the same thing: They obtain one reading from a Keithley Instruments 619 Electrometer/ Multimeter whose address switch is set to address 6. Programs are listed for the PET/CBM 2001 and APPLE II, which were at one time considered solely personal computers, the Hewlett-Packard 9825, and Tektronix 4052 terminal with 4051 GPIB Controller.

PET/CBM 2001

To run the following program after it is entered, the operator types RUN, then presses the Return key. The display will read "TEST SETUP." To program the 619 for the 2-V range and take a reading, type in F0R2X and press Return. The display will read NDCV + 0.00000E + 00 for 0 V in. Note that the output is in exponential form.

10 OPEN 6,6,1	Open file 6, primary address 6, secondary address 1.
20 INPUT "TEST SETUP";B$	Enter programming command. (e.g., 2V range = F0R2X)
30 PRINT #6,B$	Output to GPIB
40 INPUT #6,A$	Read 619 data from GPIB

50 IF ST = 2 THEN 40	If timeout, try again
60 PRINT A$	Print 619 data
70 GO TO 20	Repeat

Apple II

To run the following program on the Apple II after entry, enter RUN. The display will again read "TEST SETUP" and one must enter FOR2X to set the 619 to the 2-V range.

10 DIM A$ (20), B$(20)	Dimension data string
20 PRINT "TEST SETUP"	
30 INPUT B$:PR#3	Enter programming command (FOR2X = 2-V range)
40 PRINT "@&:@;"CHR$(97);":";	Primary address 6, secondary address 1
50 PRINT "'"; B$ "'";	Text mode; to output B$
60 PRINT "@?F:@"; CHR(97); ":";	Talk
70 PR#0	Set I/O to CRT
80 INPUT A$	Input to CRT from GPIB
90 IN#0	Set I/O to keyboard
100 GO TO 20	Repeat

The Apple II in this example uses a California Computer Systems IEEE Interface. The display will read NDCV + 0.00000E + 00 for 0 V in.

HP 9825A

The 9825A in this example used a 98034A HPIB Interface and a 9872A extended I/O ROM. The procedure is similar to that for the other two computers, except that one will press the Cont key after entry of the 619 range data.

0 dim A$[20], B$[20]	
1 dev "Emma",70601	Substitute "Emma" for the 619 primary address 6 and secondary address 01 (619 channel A)

2 rem "Emma"	Remote the 619
3 ent "TEST SETUP",B$	Enter programming command output
4 wrt"Emma",B$	Programming command to 619 over GPIB
5 red "Emma",A$	Read 619 data and assign to A$
6 prt A$	
7 gto 2	

The printer will read NDCV + 0.00000E + 00 for 0 V in.

Tektronix 4052/4051

To run the following program, type in RUN on the terminal. The remainder of the steps are similar to those described for the other computers.

5 PRINT @ 37,0:10,255,13	
10 PRINT "TEST SETUP"	
20 INPUT A$	
30 PRINT @6,1:A$	Program the 619
40 INPUT %6,1:B$	Read in 619 data over GPIB
50 PRINT B$	
60 GO TO 10	

Most of the computers use INPUT commands to input the data and PRINT to output data to the GPIB. The 9825A uses red to read in data and wrt to output bus data. (Programs courtesy of Keithley Instruments, Inc.)

STIMULI

The requirements for obtaining a test signal output from a stimulus somewhat parallel those of measurement devices in that the device must first be set up to provide the output. In a number of devices, the act of setting up the device also triggers it to provide the required output. The following routine ("Swpout") programs a function generator to provide a square wave sweep output that is incremented in frequency in 1-kHz steps from 3 to 99 kHz. The program is written in BASIC for a Hewlett-Packard 9835 desktop computer.

```
425 Swpout: !Waveform Sweep
435 DIM Freq (6)
455 A$ = "100KM1K"
465 OUTPUT 701;"C + 4KB 1F3000E + 3KA0200E0KD"&A$!Init Frq = 3KHz
475 CALL Mux (2,"3")
485 READ Freq (*)!Begin Sweep
495 Lofrq = Freq(3)
505 FOR Loop = 1 TO 7
515 Lofrq = Lofrq + 1000
525 OUTPUT 701;"F"&VAL$(Lofrq)&"E + 3K"!3 – 9KHz Sweep
535 NEXT Loop
545 Medfrq = Freq(6)
555 FOR Loop = 1 TO 90
565 Medfrq = Medfrq + 100
575 OUTPUT 701;"F"&VAL$(Medfrq)&"E + 4K"!10 – 99KHz swp
585 NEXT Loop
595 !End Sweep; Disconnect Waveform Gen
605 OUTPUT 718;"DS"
615 DATA 212, 6.5,.970,2000,34.2,88,900
625 RETURN
```

Lines 455 and 465 set up two equipment parameters. Line 455 initializes the value of dc offset voltage of the generator output. Line 465 sends a message that sets up the generator to provide a 3-kHz square wave to begin the sweep. The center portion of the message (F3000E + 3K) sets the frequency.

Line 475 calls a subroutine that utilizes the switching system to connect the generator output to the required UUT pin. Line 485 and 495 read the value 2000 from the data list in line 615 to set the beginning of the sweep process. Lines 505 through 535 form a loop that increments the frequency in 1-kHz steps from 3000 to 9000 Hz. The command & VAL$(Lofrq)& substitutes the value for Lofrq in the string sent to the generator.

Note that in line 525, the routine sends only the frequency to the generator. This particular generator retains its setup values. It changes only those values that the controller instructs it to change rather than require a complete setup each time it receives a command. Note also that the program executed an extra loop, since it originally set up the generator for 3000 Hz in line 465. The first time through the loop, the value 2000 from the DATA statement was added to 1000 in line 515 to give the first frequency, 3000 Hz. The DATA value could have been set to 3000 so the generator would increment to 4000 Hz the first time through the loop.

Lines 545 through 585 form another loop that increments the frequency from 10 to 99 kHz, again in 1-kHz steps. Line 605 disconnects the switching system (device 718) and line 625 returns control to the main program.

SWITCHING SYSTEM

The third programmable type of device in ATE is the switching system. The programmer must assure that the switching system makes the correct connections to the UUT and other devices in the ATE system. The following is an HPL subroutine that sets up an Autex FX30 coaxial scanner to interconnect the DMM input to the UUT connector.

```
0: "SCAN":
1: "Calling seq":
2: "cll 'SCAN' [UUT PIN# TO DMM +, UUT PIN# TO DMM − ]":
3. if p1*p2 = 0;gto"SCANCLR"
4: if p0#2 or p1>60 or p2>60; gto "SCANERR"
5: clr "SCANR";wait 100
6: fmt fz2.0;wrt "SCANR",
   "SA1", S[p1], "000ST"
7: clr "SCANR"; wait 100
8: fmt fz2.0;wrt "SCANR",
   "SB1",R[p2],"000ST"
9: wait 100; ret
10:"SCANCLR": clr "SCANR";
   wrt "SCANR","SA199990ST"
11:clr"SCANR";wrt "SCANR",
   "SB199990ST"
12:ret
13:"SCANERR: dsp"ERROR IN SCAN CALL";stp;ret
```

Line 0 gives the label of the subroutine, SCAN. The next two lines are comments that give instructions on calling this subroutine from the main program. These comments allow a programmer to use the routine later without searching the main program for examples to reason out how it should be done.

The parameters passed from the main program are designated p1 (the UUT pin to DMM + connector) and p2 (DMM − connection). The parameter p0 equals the number of pass parameters (in this case, 2).

Line 3 checks whether either of the pass parameters (i.e., UUT pin numbers) is set to 0. If so, the routine branches to a subroutine that sets in a default value for the scanner channel. Line 4 detects the following error conditions:

1. The number of pass parameters, p0, equals something other than two.

2. Either of the two UUT pin numbers (p1 or p2) exceeds 60. If that condition is true for either of the three conditions, the routine branches to an error routine that displays an error message.

Line 5 clears the scanner. Line 6 sets the A channel of the scanner to connect the first UUT pin number to the DMM + connector. Line 8 does the same thing for the DMM − connector. It would be helpful to review the discussion of the FX30 software requirements in Chap. 5 to make this example more meaningful.

ICT TEST PREPARATION PROGRAM

Manufacturers of in-circuit test systems provide software that assists the user in preparing test programs. The user provides certain data and the software package uses this data to generate the test program. For a circuit board, the user may provide the following information:

1. The location and type of each device

2. The interconnections between the devices or the test nodes where the measurements must be performed.

3. The input and output pins of the device.

The software may draw on the information on each device in its device library to create a final test program. The user can then run the program with a good board to give the test program an initial checkout. (This action alone, as will be seen later in the chapter on software reliability, will never adequately check out a program.)

Hewlett-Packard's 3060A Board Test System (shown in Fig. 6-1) comes with a test program preparation software package. The commands were covered in the previous chapter on ATE software. The following summarizes the commands:

group: Allocates memory space for information on the device

assign: allots receivers or drivers

apply: initiates test patterns to the drivers

receive: assigns receiver data to a variable for device subroutines

An example test program for the HP3060A is shown in Fig. 6-2. It has been divided into various functional sections to make it easier to follow. The first section of the program covers the group and assign statements that allocate memory space and assign drivers and receivers to the various nodes. The first statements, identified as "driver groups," assign and group the drivers. The second portion ("receiver groups") assigns memory space and allocates receivers to the various nodes.

The main program generates the stimuli for the test by applying the input

Fig. 6-1 The HP3060A Board Test System. The 9825 controller is at the right.

patterns as shown on the DATA and EXTD driver groups. The third statement in the main program is a gsb (Go To Subroutine) command that calls the subroutine "LT" (Logic Test). This statement puts the response of each IC into the array A$, then calls the subroutine that tests the IC involved. The first two statements

> receive"","U4A","X",A$
> if '2to4';wrt M, "U4A failed",A$

will test a 2-to-4 decoder. The receive statement places the data from the decoder input and output pins into variable A$. The second statement passes the value of A$ to the device subroutine that tests the 2-to-4 decoder. If the subroutine indicates a failure, the statement will provide an error message to the operator. Since the error message identifies the defective device, the operator can easily specify the corrective action (replace U4A).

Fig. 6-3 illustrates the flowchart for the "2 to 4" subroutine. Fig. 6-4 shows the subroutine itself. As shown, A$ contains a string of bits that gives the status sensed by the receiver at each pin. The order for the various pin states is as follows:

A$ = G(enable), B(input 1), A(input 2), Y3(output 3) through Y0

The first statement in the subroutine checks the status of the enable (G) pin. The statement A$(x,y) checks the status of bits x through y in a string.

```
"Driver Groups":
group"EXTD", "D", 1, 8
assign"EXTD", 73. 1833, 72. 1733, 71. 1633, 70. 1533
assign"EXTD", 69. 1433, 68. 1333, 67. 1233, 66. 1133
group"DATA", "D", 1, 8
assign"DATA", 26. 0733, 25. 0633, 24. 0533, 23. 0433, 22. 0333
assign"DATA", 21. 0233, 20. 0133, 19. 0033

"Receiver Groups":
group"ABUS", "R", 1, 16
assign"ABUS", 18. 3134, 17. 3034, 16. 2934, 15. 2834, 14. 2734
assign"ABUS", 13. 2634, 12. 2534, 11. 2434, 10. 2334, 9. 2234
group"U4A", "R", 1, 7
assign"U4A", 81. 2532, 15. 2834, 14. 2734, 76. 2732, 77. 2832, 78. 2932
assign"U4A", 79. 3032
group"U4A", "R", 1, 7
assign"U4B", 85. 0036, 8. 2134, 7. 2034, 86. 0136, 87. 0236
assign"U4B", 88. 0336, 89. 0436
  :     :
  :     :
apply"DATA", "(10010101)"
apply"EXTD", "(10101010)"
gsb"LT"
receive"", "ABUS", "1001010110010101", A$
if flg11; "U1 failing address out ">T$; ref
  :     :
  :     :
"LT":
receive"", "U4A", "X", A$
if '2to4'; wrt M, "U4A failed", A$
receive"", -1, "U4B", "X", A$
if '2to4'; wrt M, "U4B failed", A$
```

Fig. 6-2 Example of a test program for the Hewlett-Packard model 3060A Board Test System. (*Courtesy of Hewlett-Packard Company.*)

A$(x,x) would check the bit in position x only. If the enable is a 1, the truth table in Fig. 6-4 shows that the outputs should all be logic 1. The second step in the program checks that bits 4 through 7—the output bits—are all 1.

If the routine detects anything other than 1111, it sets a flag with the sfg command and returns control to the main program. The main program will sense the failure flag and print out a failure message. If the ouput is 1111, the next program line returns control to the main program without setting a failure flag.

The routine skipped to the fourth program line when it tested the enable and found it to be 0. The following table should make the next section of the routine easier to understand:

Input		p2	10^{p2}	A$(4,7)
B	A			
0	0	0	0001	1110
0	1	1	0010	1101
1	0	2	0100	1011
1	1	3	1000	0111

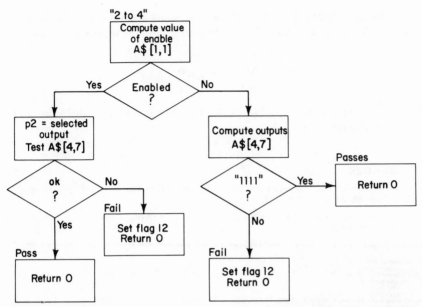

Fig. 6-3 Flowchart for a "2 to 4" subroutine. (*Courtesy of Hewlett-Packard Company.*)

The fourth line of the routine adds twice the value of the B input to the A input and assigns the value to p2. The value is listed above under p2. The next program line computes 10 to the p2 power, which also appears in the table. Leading 0s have been added to the computed value for clarity. The routine adds this value to the total binary output expression (A\$ 4,7).

```
"2to4":
ifA$[1,1]="0"; gto +3
ifA$[4,7]#"1111"; sfg 12; ret 1
ret0
2val(A$[2,2])+val(A$[3,3])}p2
if10^p2+val(A$[4,7]#1111; sfg 12; ret1
ret0
```

Block diagram

A\$ = G, B, A, Y_3, Y_2, Y_1, Y_0

Truth table:

Inputs		Outputs			
Enable	Select	Y_3	Y_2	Y_1	Y_0
G	B A				
1	X X	1	1	1	1
0	0 0	1	1	1	0
0	0 1	1	1	0	1
0	1 0	1	0	1	1
0	1 1	0	1	1	1

Fig. 6-4 The "2 to 4" subroutine and truth table. (*Courtesy of Hewlett-Packard Company.*)

As can be seen from the table, these two sums should equal 1111. The second table entry, for example, would give the following computation:

$$
\begin{aligned}
10^{P2} &= 0010 \\
A\$\ 4{,}7 &= \underline{1100} \\
\text{Sum} &= 1111
\end{aligned}
$$

If the result equals anything but 1111, the routine sets the failure flag and returns to the main program.

REFERENCES

Anunson, Robert L.: "2nd-Generation GPIB Equipment Offers Easy-to-Use Improvements," *EDN*, Aug. 19, 1981, pp. 165–172.

Dacier, William C.: "Software Generates Tests for Complex Digital Circuits," *Electronic Design*, Oct. 28, 1982, pp. 137–146.

Jackson, Trudi, and Paul Vais: "Test LSI Boards Functionally on an In-Circuit Tester," *Electronic Design*, Oct. 29, 1981, pp. 137–144.

Raymond, Douglas W.: "In-Circuit Testing Comes of Age," *Computer Design*, Aug. 1981, pp. 117–124.

Static Digital Testing, Application Note 309-1, Hewlett-Packard, Feb. 1981, pp. 2–14.

Stover, Allan C.: "Software Simulation Techniques Improve ATE Quality," *Proceedings of the ATE Seminar/Exhibit*, June 1982, pp. IV-17–IV-28.

Wharton, John: "Incoming Test Techniques for Single-Chip Microcomputers," *ATE Seminar/Exhibit Preview Guide, Electronics Test*, May 1982, pp. 62–70.

7
UUT FAULT LOCALIZATION AND DIAGNOSTICS

The first task of most ATE systems is to test UUTs. If the ATE system design and software are designed correctly, the ATE system should test the UUT and determine whether it is operating properly. If the UUT passes the test, the ATE system will display or print out a pass indication. The operator can assume that the UUT is error-free for that level of testing and send it on to the next level of production or testing.

UUT FAILURES

If the UUT fails the test, it probably did so because a fault exists within it. For example, a subassembly could have a defect in wiring, one of its components, or one of the circuit boards. A circuit board could have the following defects:

1. Bare board open or short circuits

2. Solder-caused short circuits, often due to splashes during insertion of components and to poor solder connections

3. Components that are incorrect, misoriented, out of tolerance, or otherwise defective

Many ATE systems can localize the fault based on the information generated during the test. An in-circuit tester, for example, will test board devices individually. If one is defective, the ICT will sense a failure and print a message stating that the device it just tested failed the test. The operator can return the board to assembly personnel to have the component replaced. The fault message can be attached to the defective board to identify the faulty component. This procedure frees the operator of the need to write a fault report.

In other instances, fault diagnosis becomes more complex and may require the intervention of the operator. If a driver and five gate inputs connect to a node that is found to be faulty, for example, how does one locate the defective device? Either the drive output or one of the gate inputs could be sinking current. The problem becomes even more complex when troubleshooting microprocessor circuits with bidirectional buses and large amounts of data flow. If a circuit fails, the ATE system often switches from the testing program to a diagnostic and fault-localization program that instructs the operator to probe at various points in order to narrow in on the defect.

FAULT-LOCALIZATION TECHNIQUES

ATE manufacturers have developed a number of techniques for diagnostics and fault localization. Many of them involve a guided-probe technique, in which the ATE software analyzes the fault and displays probing instructions to the operator. The software may operate with circuit data previously input to the test-preparation program, as well as diagnostic information that the test engineer provided during program preparation. If the software is written properly, an operator with a minimum of training can locate the fault.

In other instances, the test engineer or ATE personnel must write the fault localization program in its entirety. The test program often jumps to the diagnostic routines if a failure is encountered or the operator wants to use the routines to find a fault. If the routine is called when the ATE system encounters a failure, it can be assumed that the fault exists in either the section that failed or in a related section. This assumption will allow the fault to be found with fewer steps than a general troubleshooting program that starts at the beginning and assumes the fault can be anywhere.

A number of fault-localization programs use signature analysis. This technique can isolate causes of bus-related failures. If an incorrect signature is found, the node with the defective signature fails and the program directs the operator to check previous circuits' signatures. One method of localizing a fault on a bus is to use the enable lines for the various chips as start-stop inputs to the signature analyzer, then check the signatures on the bus. The signatures that are obtained will relate to the data from that chip. One could connect the chip enable for a ROM to the start-stop, for example, then check the signature of each data line. The unique signatures would relate to the operation of the ROM.

GENRAD FUNCTIONAL DIAGNOSTICS

GenRad has developed diagnostics for its functional test sets that combine diagnostic hardware and software. The 1796 Functional Test System utilizes the information contained in its CAPS X test software as an input to the diagnostic routines. The system has the capability of diagnosing both analog and digital faults. CAPS will switch to the appropriate subsystem, depending on the nature of the fault.

As with a number of ATE systems, the 1796 first localizes the fault to the node, then utilizes other techniques to narrow it down further to the pin of a chip. Fig. 7-1 shows two techniques that GenRad uses, the Straight Probe and Smart Probe. Both are guided-probe techniques that take the operator back to the failing node.

The Straight Probe software technique directs the operator to move a probe or IC clip step-by-step from the failing output to the faulty node. The Smart Probe software utilizes information that was generated during test preparation to reduce the number of probings that the operator must perform.

Another portion of CAPS X, Conditional Connectivity Probing, improves fault localization when a number of items connect to a faulty bus node, a common occurrence. This feature determines which device was the driver during the test, then directs the operator to start probing at that point. The system also has a Fast Shorts Check that uses the IC clip to check for shorts automatically between the pins, to ground, and to V_{cc}.

Fig. 7-2 shows the hardware portion of the 1796 diagnostic system, the Diagnostic Resolution Module (DRM). The system software calls up DRM when it has identified the faulty node. DRM includes a 40-pin IC clip and a current-injecting microvoltmeter probe, which operates under computer control. CAPS X determines which of the two the nature of the fault requires, then directs the operator accordingly. If a broken connection is likely, the software will direct the operator to check the signal at both sides of the open circuit. If a defective IC is likely, the software will call up its current-tracing routine and instruct the operator to check around the defective node with the microvoltmeter probe.

FLUKE AUTOMATED SYSTEMS 3050A DIAGNOSTICS

The 3050A Digital/Analog ATE System is a comparison tester that utilizes the inherent data on the reference board to aid in fault localization. The system comes with two 16-pin logic clips and two logic probes to monitor and compare circuit nodes on the UUT and reference boards. Its Diagnostic Management System (DMS) software contains two software subsystems, Autotrack and Command Table.

An operator with minimal training can use Autotrack to locate nonbus faults. Autotrack is a troubleshooting algorithm that uses guided-probe techniques to walk the operator back to the fault. The software displays the probing messages and afterward prints out the identity of the faulty device.

The 3050A first compares the UUT with the reference board to locate

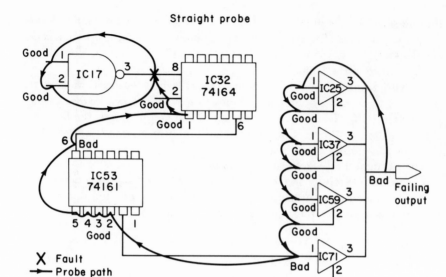

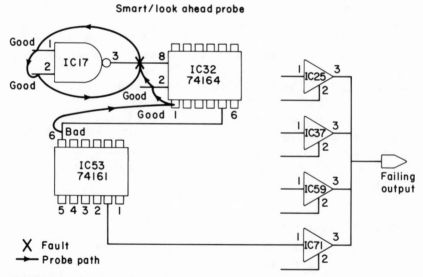

Fig. 7-1 GenRad 1796 Functional Test System techniques to narrow faults down to the pin of a chip. The Straight Probe technique guides the operator back from the failing output pin to the bad node. The Smart/Look Ahead Probe reduces the number of probings through the use of test preparation information. (*Courtesy of GenRad, Inc., Concord, Mass.*)

Fig. 7-2 The GenRad 1796 Functional Test System. The Diagnostic Resolution Module is at the right. (*Courtesy of GenRad, Inc., Concord, Mass.*)

the faulty node. Autotrack then takes over and uses board-edge and circuit-interconnection information to determine the walk-back path from the faulty node.

In order to perform diagnostics, Autotrack requires that certain information be on hand in the following files:

1. IC Type Location Cross Index File: This file gives the type number and location of each chip. A sample entry is

   E6,L7,H6 = 7400
   B1 = 7406
   .
   .
   .

2. IC Type Definition File: This file identifies the basic topology of each IC, including number of pins, location of power and ground pins, and the output pins and which input pins affect them. A sample entry is:

   14,14V,7G:7400
   = 3,2,1
   = 6,4,5
   = 8,9,10
   = 11,12,13

3. From-To Interconnect File: This file gives the board interconnections. A sample entry is:

   0-57 = D6-11
   D6-10 = C6-2,C6-10

If the failure is bus-related, DMS stops testing and switches to Command

Table. The step at which the fault occurred is retained in the test program and is used to narrow in on the fault. The system can store 256 data points around the point where the failure occurred and use that information to locate the fault. Command Table will guide the operator to the fault by displaying messages to clip or probe nodes on the UUT and reference board in order to compare the signals. The system can also activate the micro-voltmeter and direct the operator to probe toward the pin that is acting as a sink or as a source of current.

Fig. 7-3 shows a flowchart and DMS routine to troubleshoot a circuit with an 8080 microprocessor and related chips. The routine uses the DMS commands IF, ELSE (EL), END (EN), and DISPLAY (DI). If the IF condition is true, the program will execute the THEN (TH) statement that follows it.

The first levels of the flow determine if the failure is on the data bus. If so, DMS is executed. Otherwise, the routine branches to Autotrack. The first decision point in the sequence determines the direction of the data bus by checking the status of the DBIN status line from the 8080.

The routine in Fig. 7-3 begins at this point. One may find it instructive to follow through the routine with reference to the flowchart.

If DBIN is high, data is being read into the 8080 and the sequence continues downward in the flowchart. Otherwise, the program branches off to the 8080 DMS Command Sequence software. The next decision point determines whether memory is enabled. If the MBUSY status line is a 0, the memory is enabled and the sequence continues downward. The next decision point requires that the address bus be decoded to determine the type of memory device. If it is a RAM, the sequence branches to the DMS RAM Command Sequence. If it is a ROM, the routine determines which one is enabled and guides the operator with probing instructions to the pins of that ROM.

SIGNATURE ANALYSIS

Many circuit schematics have voltage levels and oscilloscope patterns at key points. These troubleshooting aids assist the technician in locating a fault. One can start from the output or in the suspected area of the fault and probe at various points until the fault is located. This method has been used for years in electronics.

The same techniques can be used for signature analyzers. Fig. 7-4 shows a circuit diagram with signatures at key points. The signature 086F should be displayed on the signature analyzer if its probe is touched to U41, pin 3. If that signature is incorrect, a fault exists at some point prior to that pin. One can then probe at pin 1. If that signature is correct and the ACLK clock signal is correct, then U41 is defective.

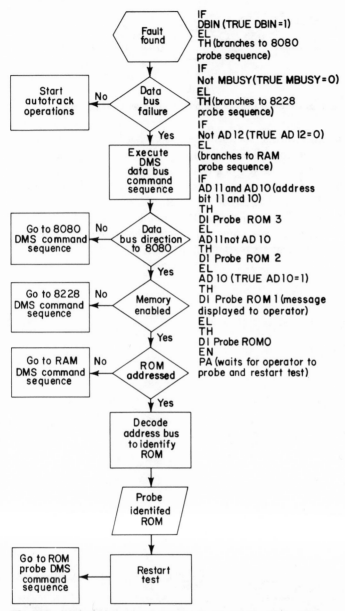

IF
DBIN (TRUE DBIN = 1)
EL
TH (branches to 8080
probe sequence)
IF
Not MBUSY(TRUE MBUSY = 0)
EL
TH (branches to 8228
probe sequence)
IF
Not AD 12 (TRUE AD 12 = 0)
EL
(branches to RAM
probe sequence)
IF
AD 11 and AD 10 (address
bit 11 and 10)
TH
DI Probe ROM 3
EL
AD 11 not AD 10
TH
DI Probe ROM 2
EL
AD 10 (TRUE AD 10 = 1)
TH
DI Probe ROM 1 (message
displayed to operator)
EL
TH
DI Probe ROM0
EN
PA (waits for operator to
probe and restart test)

Fig. 7-3 DMS routine that locates a faulty device. The routine on the right follows the flowchart, beginning at the decision "Data bus direction to 8080?" (*Reprinted with permission from Electronic Design, vol. 28, no. 13; copyright Hayden Publishing Co., Inc., 1980.*)

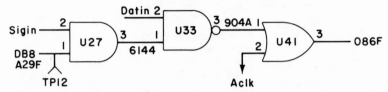

Fig. 7-4 Circuit diagram showing the inclusion of signatures at key points.

A number of manufacturers, such as Hewlett-Packard, include signature information in a number of different forms in their service manuals. Fig. 7-5 illustrates one method, the use of a troubleshooting flowchart. Note the instructions in the lower right-hand corner, regarding setting the signature analyzer START, STOP, and CLOCK inputs in order to obtain the signatures shown. The flowchart itself covers the circuit of Fig. 7-4. The first instruction tells where the three inputs must be connected to get the correct signatures. All signature analysis methods must cover the settings of START,

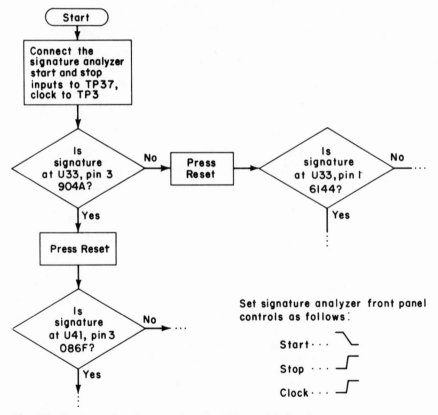

Fig. 7-5 Signature flowchart used as an aid in troubleshooting.

STOP, and CLOCK controls and where the three input lines must be connected.

The first probing asks if the signature at U33, pin 3 is 904A. If so, one presses reset and continues on to U41. If not, the signature indicates that a fault exists prior to that pin. The troubleshooter presses reset, then probes for the signature at pin 1 of U33.

The manufacturer can also list the signature for each pin of interest for the devices. The following is an example of such listings:

U27	1	A29F
	3	6144
U33	1	6144
	3	904A
U41	1	904A
	3	086F

The troubleshooting technique known as half-splitting is as useful for signature analysis troubleshooting as it is in troubleshooting of other types of circuitry. With half-splitting, the technician selects a point approximately halfway between input and output, rather than beginning at the output. If that signature is incorrect, the troubleshooter selects a point halfway between there and the input and probes there. If the signature is correct, the troubleshooter selects the probing point halfway between there and the output. This process of probing at the halfway point continues until the fault is located.

The methods described here are used manually by personnel using a signature analyzer. It should be noted that one uses many of the same techniques during ATE fault localization.

LOGIC ANALYSIS

UUT troubleshooting can be complicated by large amounts of data. One cannot always use the conventional tools, such as oscilloscope and meter, to locate glitches, buried software errors, and other such difficulties. A system with a microprocessor and STD-100 bus would be difficult to troubleshoot with conventional instruments, as would a UUT that has a serial bus such as the RS-232C. Such situations require an instrument that will allow one to monitor the state of the data lines and observe the data in a meaningful format.

An instrument suited for such monitoring is the logic analyzer, which can display the status of data lines in a number of convenient formats. Two types of logic analyzers are generally available, the timing analyzer and the state analyzer. A number of logic analyzers feature both capabilities. With such hardware problems as glitches and timing errors, one would generally choose a timing-analyzer capability. With software problems one would choose a state analyzer.

Logic-Timing Analyzer

The timing analyzer displays the status of each data line in a format similar to an oscilloscope display. The display of an eight-line timing analyzer resembles that of an eight-channel oscilloscope, except that the analyzer may show an idealized display with squared pulses. Fig. 7-6 shows the display of a logic analyzer being used in the timing analyzer mode. Many logic analyzers also capture glitches and display them as intensified marks or in some other distinctive format.

The triggering of the logic analyzer is also distinctive, in that one can trigger the sweep on a particular data word on the lines. One would select a particular combination of 1s, 0s, and "don't cares" on the input lines as a trigger and thereby close in on a troublesome occurrence. Some analyzers allow triggering on a glitch itself.

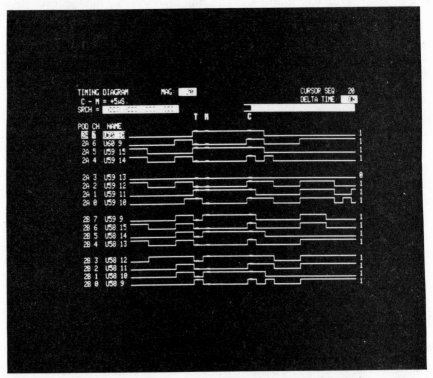

Fig. 7-6 Display of a logic timing analyzer. (*Courtesy of Tektronix, Inc.*)

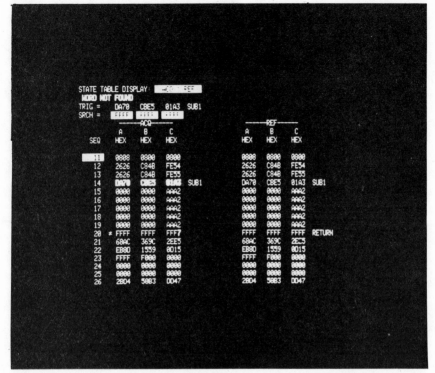

Fig. 7-7 Display of a logic state analyzer. (*Courtesy of Tektronix, Inc.*)

Logic-State Analyzer

The state analyzer monitors and displays the words on the data bus rather than the state of individual lines. Each clock pulse brings in a data sample., The analyzer will display the data in any of a number of formats, including binary, octal, and hexadecimal. Some state analyzers will display the results in the mnemonics of a particular microprocessor. Fig. 7-7 shows the display of a logic-state analyzer.

State analyzers often allow one to trigger on a particular sequence of states in order to close in on a troublesome area. The internal memory will store a number of samples, with the trigger words at the beginning, end, or middle of the samples. One can then scroll through the data samples and pick out any errors.

Tektronix DAS 9120 Logic Analyzer

Fig. 7-8 shows the DAS 9120 being used as a state analyzer. It also has timing state capability. It displays information in three colors—red, yellow,

Fig. 7-8 Tektronix DAS 9120 Logic Analyzer being used in the state analyzer mode. (*Courtesy of Tektronix, Inc.*)

and green—to differentiate between the various types of information. The display color codes the prompts, cursors, and error messages in red, for example. It displays the acquired state and timing data in yellow and any glitches in green.

A number of plug-in modules are available with the DAS 9120. Capabilities from 104 channels of data at a rate of 25 MHz to 8 channels at 660 MHz are available. An optional magnetic tape drive allows one to load and store setup data for the system. Logic-state mnemonic capabilities are available on tape for the Z80, 1802, 6800, 6802, and 8085, as are formats for ASCII, EBCDIC, and GPIB.

Two "delta time" cursors can be set at two separate events on the timing display. The analyzer will display the time difference between the two cursors. One can thus resolve timing problems to nanosecond resolution.

REFERENCES

Cassas, Don: "ATE System Finds Dynamic Faults in Real Time," *Electronic Design*, June 21, 1980, pp. 79–83.

Dynamic Digital Board Testing, Application Note 308-1, Hewlett-Packard, Nov. 1980, pp. 16–18.

Lorentzen, Robert: "Troubleshooting Microprocessors with a Logic Analyzer System," *Computer Design*, Mar. 1979, pp. 160–164.

Natrasevschi, Alfred: "SA Attacks Board Faults without Extra Hardware," *Electronic Design*, Oct. 11, 1980, pp. 191–195.

Piubeni, Steven C.: "Digital Troubleshooting with Signature Analysis," *BYTE*, Sep. 1982, pp. 466–474.

Runyon, Stan: "Instruments '80," *Electronic Design*, Oct. 11, 1979, pp. 68–79.

————: "Testing LSI-Based Boards: Many Issues, Many Answers," *Electronic Design*, Mar. 15, 1979, pp. 58–66.

Sacher, Eric: "Beyond-the-Node Fault Isolation Techniques," *Proceedings of the ATE Seminar/ Exhibit*, June 1982, pp. III-1–III-6.

Sharrit, David: "Team Up a μP with Signature Analysis and Ease Troubleshooting in the Field," *Electronic Design*, Jan. 4, 1979, pp. 138–143.

Static Digital Testing, Application Note 309-1, Hewlett-Packard, Feb. 1981, pp. 2–7.

Stefanski, Andrew: "Free-Running Signature Analysis Simplifies Troubleshooting," *EDN*, Feb. 5, 1979, pp. 103–105.

Weisberg, Martin J.: "Designer's Guide to Testing and Troubleshooting μP-Based Products," *EDN*, Mar. 20, 1980, pp. 187–214.

8

ATE RELIABILITY

Few industrial developments of recent decades have improved product quality as much as ATE. ATE has revolutionized product testing, especially in the high-technology industries, such as electronics and defense. Because of its high speed, ATE can run through tests at speeds many times that of manual test sets, where technicians themselves make all connections, adjustments, and measurements, and record the test results. These functions can take several minutes for each manual test, but ATE can step through the same function in seconds.

MANUAL AND AUTOMATIC: COMPARISONS

Let's consider an example where a manual test set procedure contains the step "Disconnect the digital voltmeter (DVM) from the VOLT test point and connect it to the ANGLE OUT test point. Measure ac voltage at AN-GLE OUT and record the result." The test technician will follow each step, disconnect the cable and reconnect it, operate the DVM and read it, and record the value, all of which could take a minute or two. A quality control inspector could also follow each step and catch subtle errors in the test procedure and specifications and the errors that the technician makes.

The ATE controller, on the other hand, will have the switching system disconnect one point from the DVM input and connect another, order the DVM to read the ac voltage at its input and pass the result over the GPIB, analyze the result, then print it out. The time from the first command to the final stroke of the printer could be but a few seconds. At such speeds, one step blurs into another and faults become undetectable.

Another difference between manual test sets and ATE besides speed lies in the degree of human control. As we have already seen, technicians on manual test sets manually perform the connections, make the measurements, and do the recording, while ATE systems perform them automatically. ATE thus eliminates many of the human errors and omissions common to manual test sets. As a result, ATE gives an improvement in product quality because of this transfer of control over the critical parts of the test cycle from a technician to the ATE controller. In addition, the ATE runs consistently each time. The test results and productivity of manual test sets, on the other hand, can vary with the moods and capabilities of the technician.

ATE RELIABILITY COMPLICATIONS

ATE can present unique difficulties to those who must assure that its reliability is adequate. (As used here, the term ATE reliability refers to its ability to detect errors and faults in UUTs.) Such difficulties should concern all who are responsible for ATE, including managers, design engineers, programmers, test engineers, quality and reliability personnel, inspectors, and ATE support engineers.

One such difficulty stems from one of ATE's major advantages: the high speed at which it operates. As contrasted with manual test sets, ATE systems run through their tests faster than a human can comprehend the steps. ATE makes the connections, sets up the test equipment, and makes the measurements, all automatically at a rate too fast for a human to follow.

Another difficulty arises from a second ATE advantage: its transfer of control from the human operator to the ATE controller. With a manual test set, a test technician controls each step in the test cycle. The sequence of tests is open to observation by others, such as an inspector or support engineer. During the tests, the human subconscious of those involved can work through the steps and occasionally flag a discrepancy or note a subtle failure.

When the test technicians look at the schematic of the unit under test during troubleshooting, they may remember some connections between the UUT test points and the output connector. Those relationships will remain in their subconcious memory. During a test a few days later, they would sense that something was wrong if the test procedure called for a test point measurement at a connector pin other than that in the schematic. This could set off a chain of events that uncovers an error in either the test procedure or the schematic.

ATE Control

ATE systems differ from manual test sets in that the ATE systems perform the steps in the test cycle internally, out of sight of those concerned with the operation of the test equipment. The interconnections between a test point and a frequency counter, for example, are ordered by the ATE controller and performed internally by the switching system. The controller sends commands over the GPIB to set up the counter, which passes its measurement results on to the controller over the GPIB.

To aggravate matters, many ATE systems require only a nontechnical operator to perform UUT tests. In fact, one of the considerations of organizations that are studying the purchase of ATE is the lower level of technical ability required of the operators. Whereas an experienced technician on a manual test set builds up suspicions that can be passed on to the support engineer for investigation, the nontechnical operator will lack the background and will overlook subtle warning signs.

ATE: Pass-Fail Indications

Once the operator initiates the ATE test program, the ATE speeds through the tests in seconds. It makes its readings, transfers its data, and sends its commands—all internally. The only evidence that the UUT passed the test is normally a pass indication on a display or printout.

Such an indication fails to prove that the UUT passed the test. In fact, no one can be sure that the ATE system even ran the test at all. The program could contain an error and jump directly to the pass printout routine without executing any part of the test. No one would realize such an error existed, since the indication (a pass printout) would be the same whether the ATE system ran the test or not.

This situation is analogous to a test technician on a manual test set entering pass on the test record without running the test. Unless an observer were present at the time, no one would suspect that the technician never ran the test. (This points out another advantage of ATE. If the software is set up correctly, a technician would find it more difficult to cut short an ATE test and get the correct test record than to run the test itself.)

Such a situation has an impact on everyone associated with ATE. Quality-control inspectors, for example, cannot rely on such standard techniques as over-the-shoulder inspections with ATE. Except during troubleshooting, the operator does little more than connect the UUT to the ATE system, then activate the test program. In the few seconds or minutes that the ATE system requires for the test, the operator and inspector can only sit back, watch the flashing displays, and observe on the printout whether the UUT passes or fails. But as we have already seen, a pass indication on an ATE printout fails to prove that the UUT actually passed the test. The quality department must therefore modify its inspection techniques if it is to assure that ATE systems test products as they are required to do.

Engineers who support manual test sets will also have to modify their practices if they are assigned to ATE. Those who support manual test sets have only to concern themselves with the reliability and operation of the hardware and the integrity of the test procedures. The test technician performs the tests manually, and the support engineer can observe each step. They can work together to uncover and resolve discrepancies in the test procedure and subtle defects in the hardware.

With ATE, on the other hand, the test is stepped through automatically at high speed and out of sight. ATE personnel can overlook defects because they remain hidden in the blur of tests and the complexities of hardware and software.

The test sequence itself lies buried in the hundreds or thousands of lines of the controller's program. If an error exists in even a single line, the ATE system could pass defective UUTs. Such an error could remain undetected in the ATE system throughout its lifetime. The long-term consequences could be catastrophic. At the least, it could cause a subtle degradation of the product. At the other extreme, it could result in a costly recall.

ASSURING ATE RELIABILITY

There is another side to ATE reliability, however. ATE is free of the human operator errors that plague manual test sets. As a result, an ATE system can remain error-free for its lifetime—once its errors have been worked out—save for the rare undetected hardware failure. The investment in time necessary to assure the reliable operation of ATE will thus pay off in the long run in improved and consistent product quality. In this effort, those responsible for the reliability of ATE must accomplish two tasks:

1. Assure the integrity of the hardware and internal operation of the ATE system.

2. Assure the integrity of the ATE software.

Both tasks will be covered in later chapters. Since the two tasks are related (i.e., the software controls the hardware operation and the hardware provides data to the controller for use in the software), personnel concerned with ATE reliability must familiarize themselves with both the ATE hardware and software. Most people associated with ATE consider themselves expert in one or the other, but they must make up their deficiencies, at least for the ATE systems for which they are responsible.

QUALITY CONTROL

In organizations that test their products on manual test sets or test benches, quality control personnel perform a number of important functions. They are generally the only group dedicated to final product quality. In order to assure that the quality is within acceptable levels, quality control inspectors can do the following:

1. Perform over-the-shoulder inspections while the technician performs the test.

2. Perform a random test of the product at intermediate and final points in the production and testing process.

3. Perform inspections of associated items, such as test records and exterior quality.

ATE Quality Control Inspection

With ATE systems, over-the-shoulder inspection may be useless. The inspector can observe that the operator plugs in the UUT and initializes the test correctly, but the usefulness of this step is questionable since the ATE software would catch most discrepancies there anyway. If the operator plugged in the UUT backwards, for example, the ATE system would fail the tests that took readings at the connector pins.

During the test, the inspector can only observe the displays and printouts and note any discrepancies there. Again, such a step could be useless since ATE personnel should have eliminated most of the obvious errors that could be found in such a check. Unless the inspectors have a significant amount of experience with the UUT and the ATE system, it is unlikely that they will uncover a significant percentage of errors.

A random test of the product could be just as fruitless. Since the production line uses ATE to test the products, the inspector may have only the option of retesting the sampled product on the same test set on which it was originally tested. Such a procedure may be useful for manual test sets, where the inspector could find errors that the technician had made. With ATE, a subtle error could mask out a UUT defect, and retesting on the same test set would cause the same defect to be masked.

Testing the UUT on another ATE system of the same type could also accomplish nothing. A design or software error would exist in both systems and would mask the UUT error in the same way.

If the quality control group possesses a manual test set or the correct test equipment, it could retest the product there and uncover any ATE system defects. Too often, however, the quality control group lacks the complex equipment necessary for the retest of the products, or the large amounts of data involved in the test require an ATE system to handle the testing.

In organizations with ATE the duties of the quality control inspector may consist of checking only those items associated with UUT quality, rather than directly checking the UUT or its testing. The inspector may perform over-the-shoulder inspections as a formality, then check test printouts and ATE logbooks for anything suspicious. In many organizations with ATE systems, they may be unable to do anything more.

ATE Quality Control Procedures

It is obvious that the quality control inspector cannot use established procedures to assure the quality of items tested on ATE. Organizations that test products on manual test sets or test benches can use such procedures, but they cannot use them for long after they change to ATE. The introduction of ATE requires a shift in emphasis in quality matters.

Some organizations assign personnel of lesser technical ability to quality groups. The use of ATE requires that the emphasis shift to quality personnel who can fathom the complexities of ATE hardware and software. These organizations must shift away from an emphasis on UUT quality and toward assuring ATE reliability, since UUT quality depends so much on the reliability of the ATE system that tests it.

Quality control personnel must become expert enough in ATE hardware and software to detect errors and faults in both. This dual capability is necessary, since defects in either one can mask out UUT defects.

Since quality control personnel may have experience with manual test sets or test benches, they may possess skills that are adequate enough to handle the hardware side of ATE, with some additional training. Because of the previous emphasis on hardware, however, quality control personnel could be deficient in software. They could thus ignore the intricacies of ATE software and concentrate on the hardware with which they are so familiar and on any obvious software errors that the test printout will reveal. Such a method is inadequate because it neglects an area that can contribute a good part of the ATE defects.

REFERENCES

McLeod, Jonah: "ATE Swings toward Merged In-Circuit, Functional Tests," *Electronic Design*, Oct. 29, 1981, pp. 90–104.

Stover, Allan C.: "Can ATE be Trusted by QC?," *Electronic Packaging and Production*, Oct. 1981, pp. 140–144 and *Electronic Production* (United Kingdom), Jan. 1982, pp. 17–21.

————: "Quality Problems with Automatic Test Equipment," *36th Annual Quality Congress Transactions*, 1982, pp. 771–776.

Weisberg, Martin J.: "Study the Life Cycle to Uncover Complex Test Problems," *EDN*, Mar. 20, 1980, pp. 177–183.

9
ATE HARDWARE RELIABILITY

The hardware of an ATE system consists of all its devices, wiring, and circuitry. An inventory of ATE hardware would include the stimuli, measuring devices, switching system, the controller and its peripherals, and the circuitry and wiring among the various portions and between them and the UUT. Few people involved with ATE have any problem identifying which items in the ATE system are hardware. They are mentioned here only to emphasize the many potential locations of ATE hardware defects.

Any part of the ATE hardware can harbor a defect so subtle that ATE test and support personnel are unaware it exists. Such a defect has the potential of masking out a UUT defect so the ATE system fails to detect it and passes a defective UUT. Since a hardware configuration is permanent unless support personnel change it, such a defect will remain in the ATE system until someone detects it and then takes action to correct it. An ATE system could thus pass defective UUTs (those that should fail a particular test but pass) throughout its lifetime unless the defect occurred often enough that the number of customer returns would point it out. Otherwise, ATE personnel would never be aware of the defect and would never have reason to investigate that section of the hardware.

ATE can contain two types of defects, called here errors and failures (or faults). Errors exist because of a mistake somewhere during the production process for the ATE, from initial planning through design, manufacture, and final checkout. Failures occur when a portion of the hardware, such as a component, breaks down during operation.

ATE HARDWARE ERRORS

Hardware errors can occur anytime from the initial planning of the ATE system until it is placed in service. Any later revisions also contain the potential for a subtle hardware error.

During initial planning and test requirement generation, for example, the UUT design engineer may overlook a UUT testing requirement. The ATE system would therefore never perform that test and could miss a UUT defect.

The UUT designer could pass on the responsibility for generating the test requirement specification (TRS) to an associate who lacks the experience to determine the UUT testing requirements with the accuracy required. The UUT design engineers could also lack experience and insight into the test techniques necessary to create an adequate TRS. Whatever the cause, someone leaves a requirement out of a document that will form the basis of the ATE design. An omission or error in an initial document can propagate throughout all later documents.

ATE Design Errors

The design of the ATE system itself can also contain errors. An obvious error would be one in which an incorrect UUT test point connects into the system. This possibility is illustrated in Fig. 9-1. If the reading at the erroneous pin corresponds to that of the original pin, the error could remain undetected. The UUT would pass those tests in which the desired test point has a failing value but the pin that connects to the ATE system has the correct value. As Fig. 9-1 shows, this situation could occur when the erroneous test point is a +5-V supply and the test requires a TTL high at the desired test point.

Circuit Errors

Errors could also exist in the circuitry itself. Fig. 9-2 shows an example in which the ATE circuitry tests for a simultaneous high at nodes A and B. The test circuit uses an AND gate. A TTL high at both inputs would produce a high at the output. As shown in Fig. 9-2b, however, the design engineer

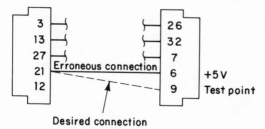

Fig. 9-1 Example of an error in the design of a cable. The designer connects pin 21 to pin 6 rather than to pin 9. Similar errors can occur during the manufacture of the cable.

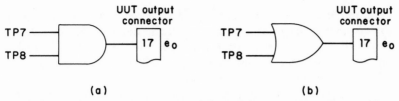

Fig. 9-2 Example of a circuit design error. In (a) the circuit is shown with an AND gate, which it requires to operate correctly. In (b), the designer used an OR gate, which will result in a PASS indication even if one of the test points fails.

erred and used an OR gate. If either test node has a TTL high, the output will be a high and the UUT will pass the test.

Fig. 9-3 illustrates another type of error. In this instance, the engineer designed a timing circuit to divide a 1-MHz timing signal down to 1 kHz. Each circuit divides by two until the desired frequency is achieved. Note that an error exists in the circuitry that divides the 125-kHz signal (Node 4). The designer rounded off the result (which should have been 62.5 kHz) to 62 kHz. The error continues and repeats at the division of 31 kHz (Node 5). The final value of 1 kHz is thus in error, in that the division shown will yield an actual frequency of 976.6 Hz, an error of 2.34 percent. As a result,

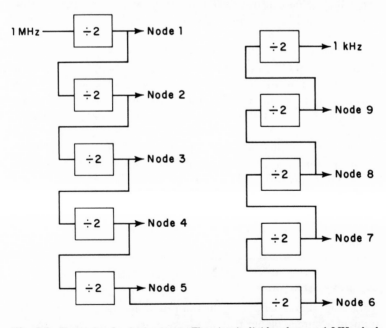

Fig. 9-3 Example of a design error. The circuit divides down a 1-MHz clock signal to 1 kHz and produces intermediate timing signals. The division is incorrect in that a series of divide-by-two circuits will give 976.6 Hz instead of 1 kHz.

the ATE system will test a UUT circuit at an erroneous frequency. Note that someone could have caught the error if the design engineer had put the intermediate frequencies on the circuit drawing. Since they were left off, anyone who saw the circuit would have had to perform the division manually in order to uncover the error.

Test Equipment Selection

Errors can also occur in the selection of the test equipment for the ATE system. If the designer selects test equipment which has ranges or accuracies that are inadequate for the UUT, the ATE system could experience errors during testing. Suppose that the TRS requires that a voltage at a UUT test point be read with an allowable error of ±0.01 percent. For 100 V, the test point can read between 99.99 and 100.01 V and be within specifications.

Suppose the designer picks a DMM that has an accuracy of ±0.01 percent, equivalent to the allowable error on the test point. For any input voltage, the DMM can give a reading that lies within ±0.01 percent of that voltage and be within specification. If the DMM reads 0.005 percent low, for example, a UUT test-point voltage of 99.994 will read approximately 99.989. The actual voltage at the UUT test point (99.994) is within specification. This result would cause the board to be diverted to troubleshooting and waste a technician's time.

If the actual voltage at the test point is 100.014 V, on the other hand, the DMM that reads 0.005 percent low will display a voltage of 100.009. The actual voltage at the test point (100.014) was out of specification. The DMM, which is reading within its allowable specification, displays a voltage that is within specification (100.009). The ATE system would thus pass a defective UUT.

In either case, the result is unacceptable. In one instance, a good UUT tested bad and resulted in a waste of troubleshooting time. In the other instance, a bad UUT was passed. The designer should have chosen a DMM with an accuracy many times (preferably 10 or more) better than the required UUT accuracies. In the above example, with a UUT accuracy of ±0.01 percent, the DMM should have had an accuracy of at least ±0.001 percent or better.

Test Equipment Accuracy

Let us consider another example to illustrate the importance of specifying a test equipment accuracy higher than the UUT requirements. Suppose one must measure RF power at a UUT output to within ±1 percent. A 100-mW output signal could thus range from 99 to 101 mW and be within specification.

Suppose also that the designer selected a power meter with a ±1 percent accuracy. If the meter measures 0.8 percent high, it would still be within specification. A UUT RF power output of 98.4 mW would be out of specification, but the power meter with a +0.8 percent error would give a reading that would be within specification.

If the designer selected an RF power meter with a ±0.1 percent accuracy, the allowable test equipment error would have less of an impact. An actual RF power reading of 98.9 mW, which is barely out of specification, would still be out of specification if read with a +0.1 percent power meter, even if the meter had a full 0.1 percent error.

Fig. 9-4 illustrates the improvement in testing that a 10 to 1 ratio in accuracy gives over a 1 to 1 ratio. The band of values that could give an erroneous reading depends on the value of e_m, or the allowable error of the measuring device. The point below which the readings can be in error due to the accuracy of the measuring device is given by the following expression:

$$y = \frac{x(1 + e_u)}{1 - e_m}$$

where y = upper limit of doubtful UUT values

x = desired value

e_u = UUT tolerance

e_m = measuring device tolerance

Since the test parameters fix the values of x and e_u, the upper limit depends on the value $(1 - e_m)$ in the denominator. As the value of e_m diminishes (i.e., the accuracy improves), the value of $(1 - e_m)$ approaches one and the band of erroneous measurements will shrink. As shown in Fig. 9-4, the band for a 1 to 1 ratio between UUT and measuring device accuracies is considerably wider than for a 10 to 1 ratio between them.

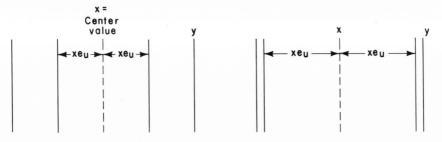

1:1 Accuracy ratio   10:1 Accuracy ratio

Fig. 9-4 Illustration of the improvement in testing that results with a 10 to 1 ratio between UUT tolerance and test equipment accuracy. A 1 to 1 ratio results in a wide range of readings of doubtful validity. A 10 to 1 ratio gives a much narrower range of doubtful readings.

Test Equipment Specifications

A design engineer could also make an error in the interpretation of test equipment specifications. A power meter specification sheet may list its specification as follows:

$\pm 1\%$ of full scale $\pm 0.1\%$ of reading

With a 300-mW input on the 300-mW scale, the meter could indicate a value with an error of ± 1.1 percent (± 3.3 mW) since full scale and the reading coincide in this instance. An input of 120 mW, however, would result in an allowable error of ± 2.6 percent, since the 3-mW error from the ± 1 percent of range specification would remain the same for all readings on that range. The allowable error would thus be the 3 mW plus the reading specification (± 0.1 percent or 0.12 mW). The total allowable error would thus be 3.12 mW. For a low-scale reading, such as 12 mW, the error could run as high as 3.012 mW, or 30.12 percent. Fig. 9-5 illustrates the error across the scale for various methods of specifying accuracy of test equipment.

The examples above point out the need to check test equipment specifications to assure that they meet UUT requirements on the ranges that will be used. The examples also point out the need to make measurements on the range just above the range that will overload the measuring device. One would thus want to make the 12-mW reading on the 30-mW range if the next lower range were 10 mW.

One can also overlook a test equipment specification that affects the accuracy of the quantity being measured. Suppose the designer specified an oscilloscope with a 50 MHz bandwidth (i.e., 3 dB down at 50 MHz). Any input signal with a frequency greater than 50 MHz could result in a further attenuation of the oscilloscope deflection and give an error. Suppose that a 60-MHz 100-mV input to a UUT is checked on the oscilloscope to see if it is the correct amplitude. Since the oscilloscope will attenuate the signal, the operator will have to increase the level to bring it up to 100 mV of

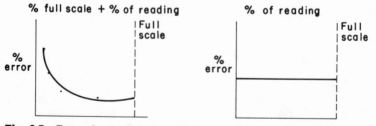

Fig. 9-5 Errors for readings across the operating range of a measuring device. In the graph on the left, the accuracy is given in $\pm \%$ full scale $+ \%$ reading. Since the accuracy in the graph on the right is given in % reading, the allowable error is constant over the entire range.

deflection. Since the increase in level only compensated for the attenuation due to the inadequate bandwidth, the input signal could now be out of specification on the high end.

It should also be pointed out that a signal just below 50 MHz could be attenuated considerably. A 3 dB or so attenuation in a signal level is considerable compared to the signal level specifications generally found in UUT tests. One should investigate such specifications as bandwidth to assure that they will meet UUT requirements. A 50-MHz bandwidth could be inadequate to set up the level of a 50-MHz signal and could be too low even to set up a 40-MHz level.

CAUSES OF DESIGN ERRORS

ATE design errors occur for a number of reasons. In most instances, human error is the cause. The UUT design engineer could inadvertently mislead the ATE designers, for example, when they ask for clarifications. The ATE designers could also misinterpret the UUT test requirements because they lack the UUT experience that would clear up subtle complexities in the TRS. Inexperienced design engineers may make errors, then overlook them during review and checkout because they lack the skills necessary to uncover subtle errors. The UUT designers may also leave certain critical details out of the TRS because they consider those details obvious.

In many ATE design organizations, engineers pass completed circuit designs back and forth for use in other projects. An error in one of the circuits could propogate into other ATE systems. Since the communications in organizations may be flawed, the discovery of an error in a circuit in one ATE system may seldom mean that the other design engineers will know of the same error in their circuits. Other engineers who have used that circuit may assume that all bugs have been worked out of the design.

The designer of in-house ATE systems will sometimes borrow circuits from the UUT itself. In this instance, the communication between the ATE and UUT designers may be worse than within the organizations themselves. As a result, any error the UUT designer discovers in a circuit may never reach the ATE designer because the revision notice stays within the UUT design department. The error will thus remain in the ATE circuit.

ATE MANUFACTURING ERRORS

During the transition from design to manufacture of the ATE system, manufacturing personnel will receive a number of documents that affect ATE quality. These include schematics, wire-wrap running lists, printed circuit board layouts, assembly diagrams, cable diagrams, and manufacturing instructions. Although personnel in manufacturing (and later in test) will find the obvious errors in these documents, the subtle errors could remain undetected, and their effects will be felt for some time in ATE performance.

The variations in errors are many. A drafter may err, for example, and connect the wrong input line to a UUT test node. The person who enters a wiring list into a computer may make an error and enter an erroneous connection. Since such lists can be lengthy, design engineers may give them only a cursory check. Once the error passes the design engineer, seldom will anyone check the running list closely enough later on to catch the error.

Cable diagrams can also be in error, especially when pin numbers on the connectors are inconsistent, as shown in Fig. 9-6. The engineer or drafter might eliminate connections, make an error in a connection, reverse digits, or move the pin numbers up or down. Since ATE systems can use a number of interconnecting cables, all with a number of pins, the potential for error is significant.

Once the ATE system enters the manufacturing cycle, the design engineer often moves on to another project and loses control of the ATE system progress. The design engineer may be unable to make a meaningful contribution to ATE hardware reliability at this point, but the effect will be felt later when the engineer reenters the picture during checkout. Many circuit and hardware details will have been forgotten, for example, and one could lose interest in the ATE system because of the demands of the new project. It may be best, then, to allow the design engineer to participate to some extent in the manufacture and circuit checking of the ATE hardware.

INSTALLATION ERRORS

The installation of an ATE system could consist of little more than wheeling the console into the test area and applying power. As a result, some ATE systems will have fewer installation errors than other electronic systems.

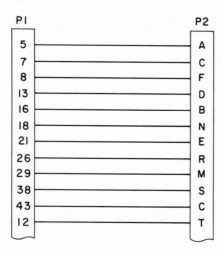

Fig. 9-6 Typical cable diagram. The pins on the two connectors may be inconsistent, which can lead to errors.

If the ATE system requires a more complex installation, the potential for error increases. With many in-circuit testers, for example, software packages give fixture layout instructions. The wiring of the fixture could result in a number of errors if either the software is defective or the person doing the wiring makes an error.

CHECKOUT ERRORS

A greater potential for errors exists during the checkout of the ATE system. This checkout may be performed in two stages:

1. An acceptance test procedure is performed on the ATE system.

2. The test program is run with a UUT to assure that the ATE hardware and software together test the UUT as they were designed to do.

A peculiar human phenomenon often occurs when the ATE system moves from design and manufacture to installation and checkout. At the risk of generalizing, the scenario is presented here. During the early stages of design, the hardware design engineers may check and recheck the designs to catch all possible errors, no matter how small. Once the ATE system enters manufacture, they may have little to do with it until it is completed, at which time it enters checkout.

In checkout, the design engineers who rechecked all the circuits for errors now change their emphasis to "getting it working and sold off." In many cases, this results from the human desire to see the project completed. The internal pressures cause them to patch up defective circuits just enough for them to seem to work according to test procedures.

Management may aggravate the situation by pressuring the engineers to complete checkout as soon as possible so the customer can be billed. The cost of an adequate checkout may also cause managers to pressure engineers to hurry. (If the engineers plunged into a checkout as detailed as the previous circuit analysis, they may have to work a significant amount of overtime.) The engineers may also dislike this alternative because it interferes with their personal lives. All of these pressures combine on the engineers and they will get the ATE system working just well enough to pass the tests and get it out the door. In this effort, hardware and software personnel may tacitly (even, perhaps, subconsciously) pass over some sections with only a cursory checkout.

ATE FAILURES

The other type of ATE defect is called here the failure, or hardware fault, which occurs as the result or a breakdown of some part of the hardware. The most common hardware failure is probably the component failure.

Some failures are obvious; others are not. If a component fails so a node is "stuck at 1," for example, the ATE would never detect the failure if it always checks that node for a logic 1.

Unlike errors, failures can occur at any time throughout the life of an ATE system. (Errors can occur later, of course, during revisions and modifications.) ATE support personnel will catch the most obvious hardware faults, but the small ones will remain and cause problems with product quality. A later chapter will cover ATE fault localization.

REFERENCES

Reyes, W., E. St. Peter, and C. Sie: "The Reliability of Spring Probe Assemblies for Automatic Test Equipment," *Proceedings of the ATE Seminar/Exhibit*, June 1982, pp. II-8–II-20.

Robinson, John, and Bruce King: "Modular Switching System Untangles Analog Signals in Test Systems," *Electronic Design*, vol. 27, no. 18, 1979.

Stover, Allan C.: "Quality Problems with Automatic Test Equipment," *36th Annual Quality Congress Transactions*, 1982, pp. 771–776.

10
ASSURING ATE HARDWARE RELIABILITY

The best way to assure that an ATE system is free of errors is to avoid errors during design and manufacture. This may sound idealistic, but reliability can improve if those involved in the design and manufacture (as well as installation, checkout, and subsequent support) have an error-free ATE system as a goal. To do so, they would have to strive for perfection in all phases of development. A personal Zero Defects program could avoid many of the usual errors. In the end, of course, human errors will still crop up and will require a thorough checkout to locate them, but the initial efforts to keep down errors will hopefully have paid off. If so, the ATE system will go into checkout with fewer subtle errors that could affect UUT testing.

DOCUMENTATION ERRORS
Since documentation ties together many of the stages over the life of an ATE system, one can reduce errors in ATE systems by reducing errors in the documentation. A critical document for ATE is the UUT test requirement specification (TRS). The TRS will be covered here in detail, but emphasis should also be placed on other pertinent documents, such as schematics, wiring lists, etc.

The UUT design engineers base the TRS on their knowledge of the UUT circuitry and interfaces. The inputs to the TRS come from the design engineers in each specialty. For a radar antenna, for example, one engineer may write the RF portion of the TRS while another writes the data and control portion. If they prepare the TRS while they design the UUT, they will have the requirements fresh in their minds. Too often, however, they wait until months after they have completed the bulk of the design. As a result, they could overlook an important detail or two.

If possible, the design engineers should never delegate the writing of the TRS to inexperienced engineers. While this method has merit in that it does develop future TRS writers, it could result in a TRS with a number of subtle errors and omissions. If the workload requires that one of these engineers write the TRS, the UUT design engineer can list the critical UUT design specifications during the design, then use that list to check the completeness and correctness of the TRS.

Those involved must review the TRS to assure that all requirements that are critical are included, even though they may feel such details should be obvious to another engineer. Too often, engineers get so involved in their own fields, they forget how complex parts of it may be to the uninitiated.

ATE INFORMATION ERRORS

Since the TRS often lacks some necessary details of UUT operation, ATE personnel must probe deeper for the details they need to design an effective system. They may use preliminary interface documents, UUT connector information, and parts lists, and may interview the UUT design engineers.

Since ATE personnel begin their study early in a program, they often must use preliminary information to start their designs. Since the information is preliminary, the design engineers may revise it later. Unless ATE personnel have a close relationship with the design department, or a rigid distribution system exists in the organization, ATE personnel may never receive the revisions. By the time the documents have been released, ATE design engineers may have completed the bulk of their design. They will review what finalized documents they receive and make the changes they feel should be made. They may never receive some documents, of course, and will miss subtle errors that exist in the original documents. As a result, the influence of the preliminary documents will remain in the recesses of the hardware (and software) designs and could account for less noticeable errors.

ATE personnel should thus maintain a close relationship with UUT design personnel. This would be a two-way relationship since the ATE personnel require accurate information to produce an error-free design and UUT design personnel want the ATE to test their designs correctly. The organization can also set up a rigid distribution system to assure that ATE personnel receive the revisions of all pertinent documents.

Despite the close relationship between the ATE and UUT personnel, the ATE design engineer can still receive misleading or erroneous information. The stereotype of the engineer who cannot communicate with other engineers is often well-founded. To assure that they receive correct information, ATE personnel should develop an accurate technique for interviewing UUT design engineers. They should list all questions beforehand in as precise a form as possible. During the interview, they should stay on the subject, repeat important answers, summarize at key points, take notes, and give some conclusions. The notes can serve as a source of follow-up questions.

ATE DESIGN ERRORS

The ATE design engineer will undoubtedly commit some errors in the ATE design. This tendency to commit errors is human and almost inevitable, considering the complexities of humans. Design engineers, as all engineers, live and work under the influence of emotional forces that stem from family, ambition, self-worth, self-confidence, moods, attitudes, and even what seems an inherent self-destructive syndrome within us.

Despite what one might think about the "purity of design," such emotional forces influence the design process and may even subvert it. We humans are resilient, however, and can catch many of the errors we commit. Some of the subtle ones, however, will slip by us.

UNCOVERING ERRORS

Since our human traits cause our errors, we can use our traits to uncover our errors. The following are some methods of achieving this.

1. Rather than try to work with a sketchy knowledge of such necessary items as the UUT design, one should become intimately familiar with it. This knowledge will prevent many errors during design and checkout.

2. The subconscious must have time to work on uncovering discrepancies and errors. This can be done by diverting oneself from the design process. Another project or a busy vacation will wipe the mind clear of the project and stimulate the subconscious.

3. One should arrange for a design review with only the UUT design engineers in order to explain the interfacing circuitry, interpretations of the TRS, and the test methods. The UUT design engineers can assess the validity of the ATE design and test methods without the distraction of having other departments present.

4. One should seek the assistance of capable designers in reviewing doubtful portions of the circuitry. Of course, one may have to repay these designers by reviewing their designs later.

The Standard Design Review

One will note the absence of any recommendations for the standard design review so popular among design organizations. These design reviews should be held in order to bring together all persons (and only those persons) concerned with the particular ATE system. These sessions must be made meaningful, however, something which is seldom done. In the effort to make the review useful, one should invite representatives of only the departments that can make a contribution. The following are possibilities:

• Test department, which will use the ATE system.

• Logistics, which will supply the materials.

• Manufacturing, which will build it.

• Program office, which is concerned with UUT testing schedules.

• UUT design engineers.

   Unfortunately, the list too often expands to include those with only a marginal interest in the ATE system itself. Too often, also, those who can make a contribution fail to attend. The design review that could have served such a worthwhile purpose degenerates into a crowded maze of posturing, boredom, and irrelevance. (Such meetings could be a rich source of study material for a psychology thesis.) A couple of aggressive attendees may dominate the review with parochial concerns irrelevant to the ATE system itself. Others may concentrate on details that divert the review from items of more general interest.

   Since a design review can run efficiently for only a limited period of time, such dominance will deprive less aggressive attendees of the attention their areas require. The focus could thus shift away from areas in which a discussion could uncover problems. The following are some steps to improve the yield of the standard design review.

1. Limit the attendees to those who have a significant interest in the ATE system. This step will require tough decisions in eliminating a particular group. Since any group will have *some* interest in the ATE system, however slight, one must set up a standard of acceptable interest level and follow that standard in making up the list of invitees. One should then expand the list to include individuals who can make significant contributions. In order to minimize the effects of selection errors, one can send copies of the minutes to the groups and individuals who were considered but dropped before the list was finalized.

2. Select a strong moderator who will keep the meeting productive, break up side discussions, and allow everyone to make a contribution. As with any recommendations, reality seldom represents the ideal, but every attempt should be made to channel the meeting toward the desired goals.

3. Publish an agenda with starting and stopping times, then try to follow it. These steps can force the review toward the desired goals. One could ensure that the meeting ends near the desired time by setting a closing time that coincides with lunch or quitting time. This could be too restrictive, however, and limit discussions at a time when they may be productive.

4. The minutes and action items should be published and distributed to all persons involved. The designer should follow up on the action items of others to assure that they are completed.

The meeting could be scheduled from 9 A.M. to 11 A.M. as a compromise. This schedule would allow participants to get organized in the morning before the meeting starts. The 11 A.M. stop time would allow the meeting to run over before lunch in case it is productive. Once the time limit has passed, and discussion starts to lag, the moderator can take the initiative and ask for final comments from each group present. A quick reading of the action items and designated responsibilities will serve to move the meeting to a close. Such a technique will end the meeting before it becomes unproductive and wastes the time of everyone present.

GROUNDING AND LOADING PROBLEMS

Hardware designers generally concern themselves with the circuitry, GPIB, and test equipment of the ATE system. The mechanical engineers handle the mechanical aspects of the system, such as cooling, layout, and the mechanical portions of the fixture. A gap in responsibility can occur in that no one concerns themselves with such items as grounding and capacitive loading, which affect the reliability of the ATE.

Capacitive loading can affect the stimuli and measurements. It especially affects such logic families as low-power Schottky TTL with its fast rise and fall times. Capacitive loading can cause transients and glitches that cause undesirable UUT responses. Ground noise and other grounding problems come from a number of causes, including poor ground connections, ground loops, and fixture inductance, among others.

A number of methods exist to minimize grounding problems. Most of them are standard and include keeping ground leads short, using larger wires for returns, and assuring that the proper connections are made to power supply and circuit grounds.

More specialized techniques also exist. Fig. 10-1a shows a typical test circuit. The stimulus provides an input signal to the UUT while the measuring device measures the response. Note that the circulating current introduces an error voltage in the inductance and resistance in the ground path.

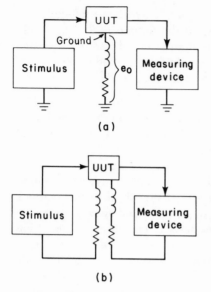

(a)

Fig. 10-1 Example of a technique to reduce grounding errors. In (a), e_o of a typical test circuit is an error voltage caused by inductance and resistance in the ground path. In (b), the use of separate ground leads reduces the effects of ground currents.

(b)

The measuring device measures a voltage that includes the expected output and the error voltage.

With a static current, the resistance will cause the greatest error. With a signal or step function, the inductance will assume greater importance. The use of separate ground leads as shown in Fig. 10-1b minimizes the effects of the ground currents. The high impedance of the measuring device would limit the ground current.

MANUFACTURING DEFECTS

Once the hardware engineers finish with their design, they turn the assembly information over to the manufacturing department for fabrication. As with the design phase, a number of techniques exist to minimize manufacturing errors. Some of these techniques concentrate on the reduction of human errors in the manufacturing process.

One must be aware of the problems that can exist throughout the manufacturing process that can cause errors. The following are some of the potential problems and some steps to minimize their effects.

1. The documents that design engineers provide to the manufacturing department may be in error. These include schematics, wiring diagrams, and running lists. The manufacturing personnel should take some time to review these documents and try to find errors. The fact that they are looking at the documents for the first time may make it possible to un-

cover errors that design engineers missed because of their familiarity with the documents. Outside of such a review and alerting manufacturing personnel to report anything suspicious, little can probably be done to eliminate documentation errors. It is to be hoped that the checkout will later uncover all such errors.

2. The manufacture of circuit boards can introduce additional errors. These errors coincidentally include many that in-circuit ATE systems will detect, including misinstallation and misorientation of parts, incorrect or defective components, and circuit board short circuits and open circuits. An ICT would catch such errors, but an organization should have a high enough volume to justify its use. Otherwise, a manual circuit check can be made, which will catch many errors. If possible, the technician should perform this check from a document other than that used for the manufacturing of the board. If the board were wire-wrapped by machine from a running list, for example, the technician could use the schematic to circuit-check the board. An effective quality control program, in which the inspectors perform board inspection and provide feedback to manufacturing on any errors discovered, will prevent many errors later in the ATE system.

3. Defects in ATE interconnecting wiring can also occur. Again, one should circuit-check the wiring from another document, if one is available.

If a defect is found to exist anywhere, one must take care in correcting it. Otherwise, another error could be introduced into the system. If an incorrect part is found on a board, for example, one could easily select another incorrect part or misorient the replacement. After all repairs have been made, the repaired circuitry, as well as all associated and adjacent circuitry, should be circuit-checked.

CHECKOUT ERRORS

Because of the intimate relationship between hardware and software in ATE systems, it is difficult to separate their checkouts. A thorough discussion of checkout errors is contained in the chapter on assuring ATE software reliability.

CALIBRATION

When the ATE system is placed into service, one must take steps to assure its long-term accuracy by performing a periodic calibration. Calibration is the act of comparing a device with a higher-accuracy standard, then adjusting to correct the difference or recording it for later correction.

The Need for Measurements

For each quantity to be measured, a measuring system provides a unit in terms of which that quantity can be expressed. Length, mass, voltage, and frequency are examples of quantities that are measured. For each, a unit or combination of units must exist that allows the amount of that quantity to be measured and expressed. An object can therefore be measured and found to be so many units length or frequency or mass.

As far back as ancient times, people had to select basic units with which to express the quantities they wished to measure. The cubit, for example, was an ancient unit equal to the length of a forearm.

It soon became apparent that such units lacked accuracy because they varied among people. It became necessary for governments to define the units better or to maintain an official representation of a unit under their control. These two methods of standardizing units are sometimes referred to as measurement standards. Their use by a society and its governments organizes the system of measurements within that society.

Early attempts to improve measurement standards included the designation of a bar of metal as the official length of the yard and the length of three barleycorns placed side by side as the English standard for the inch.

MEASUREMENT STANDARDS IN THE UNITED STATES

As the need for more accuracy in measurements grew, so did the need to improve measurement standards. This need was recognized early in U.S. history and Congress was given the authority under the Constitution to "fix the standards of weights and measures."

The need to have accurate time in the determination of longitude for the navigation of ships spurred the need for precise machine tools in the manufacture of clocks. Clockmakers improved the precision lathe in the eighteenth century for the manufacture of accurate clocks. The use of the sextant, telescope, and other scientific instruments gave an impetus to the development of accurate machining tools. The screw micrometer and the screw-cutting lathe, developed in 1800, were accurate to 0.0001 in. By 1856, machines could measure with an accuracy of 0.000001 in.

In 1798, Eli Whitney used principles of mass production to build muskets under a U.S. government contract. By 1825, the contracts of the Army Ordnance Department required that manufacturers use mass production for the assembly of firearms. This required the manufacture of interchangeable parts, which increased the need for precise and reproducible measurements.

Congress took its first step to legalize a system of measurements when it passed the Metric Act of 1866, which made it "lawful to employ the weights and measures of the metric system." Use of the metric system was voluntary, however, and still is.

International Measurement Standards

The international Convention of the Meter in Paris in 1875, which the United States and most European nations attended, established a certain platinum-iridium bar and cylinder as the official meter and kilogram for international use. These first international measurement standards were stored at the International Bureau of Weights and Measures in Sevres, France. The United States decreed in 1893 that its copies of the international meter and kilogram were the "fundamental standards" of the United States in length and mass. The establishment of the National Bureau of Standards in 1901 placed the responsibility for measurements in a single government bureau. The National Physics Laboratories in Great Britain and similar offices in other countries perform the same function.

As the need for higher accuracy progressed in this century, the National Bureau of Standards developed new measurement standards. No longer is the standard for length the meter bar, for example, but is defined as 1,650,763.3 wavelengths of radiation from the Krypton-86 atom. A standards laboratory can use this definition to reproduce the meter with the proper equipment.

International measurement standards represent the basic measurement units (volt, meter, kilogram, etc.) at the international level and have been approved by an international convention. The International Prototype Kilogram kept at the International Bureau of Weights and Measures at Sevres, France, is still recognized as the international standard for the kilogram. Other units, such as the volt, meter, and degree Celsius, are given definitions that a national bureau of standards or a standards laboratory can reproduce.

The National Bureau of Standards (NBS) is the agency responsible for measurement accuracy in the United States. NBS maintains the National Prototype Kilogram, which is sent periodically to Sevres for comparison against the International Prototype Kilogram. NBS laboratories maintain the measurement standards and equipment that reproduce other measurement units.

NBS calibrates many measurement standards found in high-level standards laboratories in the United States and abroad. These laboratories, in turn, calibrate the standards of other laboratories, who in turn use them to calibrate the test equipment of the organizations they support. The test equipment is then used to test the final products or systems.

Traceability of Accuracy

The accuracy of any product or system can thus be traced through the calibrated test and measuring equipment to the laboratory standards, higher-level laboratories, NBS, and finally to international standards. The labora-

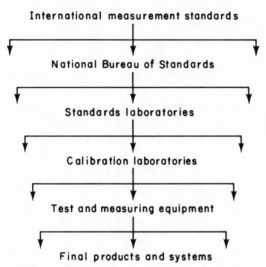

Fig. 10-2 The system of traceability. In order to assure the accuracy of measurements, the accuracy of any measurement should be traceable from the final product to an international measurement standard.

tory that calibrates test and measuring equipment is part of an intricate and internationally-accepted system to assure the accuracy of the final products. This system is known as *traceability*, which can be described as follows:

> *The accuracy of any system can best be assured if its accuracy can be traced back, step by step, to an international measurement standard.*

If the path breaks at any point, accuracy and confidence in the final product can be lost. The path will break, for example, if an organization fails to calibrate its test and measuring equipment properly. Fig. 10-2 illustrates the system of traceability.

ATE SELF-TEST PROGRAM

The ATE self-test program represents one of the fastest methods of assuring ATE performance. A self-test program generally is used for one of the following reasons.

1. Acceptance testing: The program mates hardware and controller to assure that they operate as they should and that at least part of the hardware operates as it should. Due to the nature of its use, it is written to give a thorough one-time test of the hardware. As a result, the time it requires is relatively unimportant. A streamlined version can be used throughout the life of the ATE whenever its operation is doubted.

2. Preoperational test: One can use this program at the start of work to test the ATE system. To avoid a significant delay, the test should be brief, but still thorough enough to test a worthwhile portion of the system.

3. Diagnostic: The diagnostic program can vary from a complete guided-probe package that locates the fault to a prediagnostic program that assists the troubleshooter by finding the general location of the fault. A previous chapter on UUT fault analysis covered similar diagnostic programs.

A typical self-test program would go through the following steps in one of its tests:

1. Set up various stimuli (e.g., signal generator, power supply) of the ATE system for certain output signals. The controller could set up a signal generator to provide a particular amplitude and frequency output and a power supply to provide a voltage output.

2. Set up the measurement devices (e.g., digital voltmeter [DVM], frequency counter) to measure the appropriate stimuli outputs. In the example above, the controller would set up the frequency counter to measure the frequency of the signal generator and the DVM to measure the power supply output.

3. Connect the stimuli to the measurement device through the switching system and make the measurement.

4. Read the measurement results into the controller from the GPIB, check whether they are within limits, and print out the results.

To a limited extent, self-test programs can assure the correct operation of the test equipment, switching system, controller, and some internal wiring and circuits. They could be limited in that they can check only stimuli and measurement devices that are compatible on all ranges and functions of interest. It cannot check a phase meter, for example, unless the ATE system contains a phase generator or the equivalent circuits. A low-accuracy power supply cannot check the higher accuracy of a DVM, although they can check each other's operation. One can check the frequency of a function generator if the ATE system has a frequency counter, but it may be difficult to check such parameters as waveforms (sine, square, ramp) or modulation without the intervention of the operator.

REFERENCES

Dynamic Digital Board Testing, Application Note 308-1, Hewlett-Packard Co., Nov. 1980, pp. 19–22.

Miller, Gary E.: "Noise—The Silent Killer," *Proceedings of the ATE Seminar/Exhibit,* June 1982, pp. II-21–II-27.

11

ATE SOFTWARE ERRORS

Errors that remain in ATE software can affect UUT testing for the life of the ATE system, or until someone locates and corrects the errors. Humans introduce errors into ATE software and only humans (sometimes with the aid of a software testing tool) can locate and correct them.

Such subtle errors remain buried in hundreds or thousands of program lines and are difficult to detect. A single erroneous character in a variable or a single deleted line can cause the ATE system to pass a defective UUT without test personnel being aware of the error.

SOFTWARE ERRORS

In one actual instance, a test required that a DVM measure a TTL low at a certain UUT connector pin. The program, however, directed the switching system to another pin by mistake. This pin was grounded in the system. As a result, the DVM always measured a voltage that fluctuated around 0, no matter what the voltage was at the pin of interest. A UUT that had a TTL logic high at the pin of interest (which should have resulted in a fail indication) would have passed.

As was shown in the chapter on hardware defects, such a mixup can easily occur. Perhaps pin 43 on the UUT connects to test panel pin 18, then connects through internal wiring to switching system pin 32. Pin 32 can connect through the switching system to channel 2 (if the program connects it correctly), which can connect to the DVM. With so many numbers involved, the hardware engineer can easily make an error in the list of connections. Programmers must wade through lists of such numbers and could also make an error, such as switching pins 43 and 32 in the program or reverse the digits and write down 23 instead of 32. One could minimize some errors by utilizing the method covered in an earlier software chapter which allows the programmer to use UUT pin numbers instead of switching system pin number. An error could still occur in the exchange of pin numbers.

In another instance, the test required voltage measurements at three separate test points. The program contained an error, however, and one test point was measured three times. An example of such an error is shown as follows. The routine should measure the voltages at three separate and consecutive pins: 35, 36, and 37.

```
FOR I = 1 TO 3
X = 34
X = X + 1
OUTPUT 712, "SA1",S[X],"000ST"
INPUT 705,V
PRINT V
NEXT I
```

In the above routine, the loop sets the switching system to pin 35 each time. As a result, the DVM reads and prints out the voltage at pin 35 three times in a row. If the voltage fluctuates a bit each time, the three readings will appear to have been measured at three different test points. The line X = 34 should have been before the loop. The first time through the loop, X would increment to 35 and the voltage would have been read at that pin number. The next two passes through the loop would result in X being incremented by one, so the measurements would be made at pins 36 and 37.

Programmers can make a number of errors. The following is another example of a programming error:

```
27 red 706,F
28 if F>402 or F<398;gto +3
29 prt "FREQ PASS";gto +2
30 prt "FREQ FAIL"
31 "NEXTST":
```

The history of this error will show how readily some errors can occur. The programmer wanted to correct an error in line 30 after the program had been entered into the controller. Since the controller displays an error message when an attempt is made to change the destination of a gto statement, the programmer had to change line 28 from gto +2 to gto +3. The error resulted from the failure to change the statement back to gto +2 once the statement in line 30 had been corrected. As a result of the error, the program will never give a fail indication.

At some time after the ATE system has been in use long enough for operators to become comfortable with it, an operator may notice that the system never gives a fail printout. The operator may decide to report the suspicions to the ATE support engineer for investigation, or just ignore it. The support engineer could also ignore the report or forget to investigate it. The possibility that the error remains in the program even after someone becomes suspicious is significant.

Still another type of programmer error (similar to a hardware error described in a previous chapter) is shown in the following routine:

.

.

.

```
225 red "SPEC",A
226 if A⟩=32 or A⟨=34; prt "PASS"; gto +2
227 prt "FAIL"
```

.

.

.

An error exists in line 226 in that an OR statement rather than an AND statement was used. The routine will give a pass indication for all values of A, since any value would be either greater than 32 or less than 34. An AND statement would specify that the measured value must lie between the upper and lower limits to pass.

One can easily make such an error because a similar pass-fail routine uses an OR statement. The statement below is an example:

```
if A⟨32 or A⟩34; prt "FAIL"
```

This statement would give a fail indication if the measured value were less than or greater than the specified limits.

The following routine contains another programmer error. It was discovered some years after the program was placed into use.

```
121 CALL Scan (27,21)
123 ENTER 710;A
125 IF (A⟨108) OR (A⟩120) THEN Err = 1
127 CALL Scan (33,21)
128 ENTER 710;A
130 IF (A⟨14) OR (A⟩16) THEN Er = 1
133 CALL Scan (39,21)
135 ENTER 710;A
137 IF (A⟨4.5) OR (A⟩5.5) THEN Err = 1
```

.

.

.

193 IF Err = 1 THEN DISP "SERIES FAIL"
195 IF Err = 0 THEN DISP "SERIES PASS"

Err is a variable that indicates whether any reading in a series is out of specification. If so, Err is set to a 1. The statement in line 193 checks whether the value of Err is 1. If it is, it will display a fail indication. Otherwise the program will display a pass indication.

In line 130, the programmer made an error and misspelled the fail variable as Er instead of Err. If the test in that section fails, the variable Er will be set to a 1. The variable Err will remain 0. Since lines 193 and 195 check for the value of Err, the routine will give a pass indication.

The following routine contains still another type of error:

0: "POWER SUPPLY TESTS":
1: red "DVM",V
2: if V⟩ = 87 and V = ⟨93; prt "PASS"; gto +2
3: prt"FAIL"

The programmer here is measuring 90 V at a test point. The error lies in line 2, which checks whether the measured value is within specification. The UUT test requirement specification states that the voltage at the test point shown must be within ±3 percent of 90 V to pass. The limits are in error in the routine and should have been 87.3 to 92.7 (90 ± 3 percent = 90 ± 2.7). The programmer accidentally rounded off the limits in a calculator during a computation. As a result, all UUTs with a measured value from 87 to slightly less than 87.3 and from slightly more than 92.7 to 93 V should fail, but the ATE system will print out a pass indication.

The following routine illustrates the difficulties in uncovering program errors:

425 Swpout: !Waveform Sweep
435 DIM Freq (6)
445 RESTORE 615
455 A$ = "100M1K"
465 OUTPUT 701;"C + 4KB1KF3000E + 3KA0200E0KD"&A$!Init Freq = 3 KHz
475 Call Mux (2,"3")
485 READ FREQ (*) ! Begin Sweep
495 Lofrq = Freq (4)
505 FOR Loop = 1 TO 7
515 Lofrq = Lofrq + 1000
525 OUTPUT 701;"F"&VAL$(Lofrq)&"E + 3K"!3 – 9KHz Swp
535 NEXT Loop
545 Medfrq = Freq (6)
550 FOR Loop = 1 TO 91

```
555 Medfrq = Medfrq + 100
575 OUTPUT 701;"F"&VAL$(Medfrq)&"E + 4K"!10 - 99KHz Swp
585 NEXT Loop
595 !End Sweep; Disconnect Waveform Gen
605 OUTPUT 718;"DS"
615 DATA 212,16.5,.907,2000,5000,900,900
625 RETURN
```

This routine is almost identical to a routine described in the previous chapter on ATE software. This routine should provide a square wave output from a waveform generator swept in frequency from 3 to 99 kHz. The routine contains two major errors. Line 455 sets the amount of dc offset in the output signal. The waveform generator requires the message "+ 100KM1K" instead of "100M1K" to set the correct dc offset.

Line 495 is also in error in that the statement will call 5000 instead of 2000 from the DATA list of line 615 in order to set the starting point of the sweep. The programmer introduced this error because of lack of experience with that particular function. A seemingly valid assumption (that the DATA item count begins with Freq (1) instead of Freq (0)) resulted in an erroneous starting point for the frequency sweep. The lower sweep will start at 6 kHz instead of 3 kHz. The upper sweep would have also been affected but the starting point happened to be listed twice. As a result, the upper sweep (which uses Medfrq as a parameter) will still start at 10 kHz. An error also exists in the upper sweep in that it contains a loop too many and will sweep up to 100 kHz. This may never affect the UUT testing to any extent, but the sweep could just as well have been 1 kHz less than required (which would have affected the UUT test).

Note the difficulty in uncovering an error in the above routine of only a few lines! If one had been unaware that any error existed there, they would probably have never noticed anything was wrong. Imagine the potential for subtle error in a program of hundreds or thousands of lines!

Errors can exist in any part of the program. One should take care with the code in the following areas, which have a high potential for error.

1. Specifications and limits. As we have seen, a potential exists for error in the statements that test whether a measurement is within tolerance. The following routine further illustrates this error:

```
76 wrt 705, "FREQ"
77 red 705,F
78 if F⟩ = 384 and F⟨ = 416;gto "PASS"
```

A check of the routine reveals no error. It reads a 400-Hz frequency and checks that the reading is within ±4 percent. A check with the programmer's notes will support the conclusion that the routine is free of error.

A check of the latest version of the TRS, however, will reveal that the tolerance is in error. The latest revision of the TRS requires a new tolerance of ±1 percent. The programmer never received the latest revision and therefore left the original value in the program.

The point here is that the specification errors can result from many causes outside of programmer error. An error in the TRS, the lack of a revision distribution system, or erroneous information provided by the UUT designer over the phone can all result in an error in specifications.

2. Pass-fail routines: A previous example illustrated this error. The software there set the variable Er instead of Err to a one when a failure occurred. Since the pass-fail routines check the UUT specifications, they are as critical as the specifications themselves. Any error in the pass-fail routine could mean that the UUT will pass with out-of-specification readings.

3. Commands to test equipment: Since these commands set up the test equipment, an error could mean that the test equipment is set up in error. If the program sets up a DMM on ac volts instead of dc volts, for example, the DMM could measure a value near 0 V whatever is the value of the applied dc volts. If the test happens to require a dc reading, it could pass even though the dc voltage is in error. In some cases, the commands are buried in loops and calculations which further hide errors. The previous program example for a swept frequency illustrates the use of loops and calculations to obtain the required commands.

4. Incorrect READ/DATA and array statements: The swept frequency routine also illustrates the use of READ/DATA statements and arrays to some extent. Since the DATA statement contains a list of unrelated values, one could easily make errors and have difficulties rechecking them. One can miss a value, delete a decimal point, or place an item in the wrong position. With an array, one can call up the wrong position in the array, i.e., call A\$ (6,1) instead of A\$(1,6).

5. Incorrect calculations: Programmers can introduce these errors in a number of ways. They can make errors in the interpretation of the mathematical hierarchy or symbols of the controller, make an error in the entry of the equation, or use the wrong equation.

CAUSES OF SOFTWARE ERRORS

Software errors generally originate from one of two sources. First, someone can provide erroneous information to the programmer. Perhaps the design engineer provides a tolerance that is too wide. The programmer will accept that value and test the UUT to it. It would be improbable that anyone could notice this error during a check of the program. The programmer would have to check the program against the latest version of the TRS. It should be noted that a tolerance that is too tight is also undesirable. More UUTs will fail and the technicians will waste time in troubleshooting UUTs that should have passed the test.

Throughout the design phase, departments produce a number of documents that relate in some way to the software. Programmers must use these documents, often in preliminary form, in order to begin programming early in the project. The programmers can minimize errors by using a single document (of the latest revision) from which to write the program. Most often, the TRS will serve as this document. The programmer should check the latest version of the TRS against the program to assure that any changes have been made in the software.

The second way errors get into test programs is through the programmers themselves. Whereas the documentation errors can involve a number of people, the programming errors involve one person, the programmer of that particular module.

Programmers thus introduce their individual errors into the test program. These errors strike at the ego of the programmer involved, especially when someone finds them during checkout, design reviews, walkthroughs, or, what is worse, after the ATE system has been in operation for some time. Programmers are human in that they are torn between the desire for others to uncover their errors, no matter how embarassing, and the hope that their sections of the test program will turn out to be error-free. It would be best if programmers could find their own errors. In some cases, however, they are too close to the program to see the obvious defects.

The subject of software reliability is a vast one. As the examples here indicate, a potential for disaster exists in every test program. Persons concerned with ATE software should be aware of this potential in order to prevent or eliminate the errors that will affect UUT testing.

REFERENCES

Clapp, Judith A.: "Designing Software for Maintainability," *Computer Design*, Sept. 1981, pp. 197–204.

Levin, Harold: "Enhanced Simulator Takes On Bus-Structured Logic," *Electronic Design*, Oct. 29, 1981, pp. 153–157.

Mosteller, William: "The Elusiveness of Software," *IEEE Spectrum*, Oct. 1981, p. 46.

Stover, Allan C.: "Can ATE be Trusted by QC?" *Electronic Packaging and Production*, Oct. 1981, pp. 140–144 and *Electronic Production* (United Kingdom), Jan. 1982, pp. 17–21.

————: "Quality Problems with Automatic Test Equipment," *36th Annual Quality Congress Transactions*, 1982, pp. 771–776.

————: "Software Simulation Techniques Improve ATE Quality," *Proceedings of the ATE Seminar/Exhibit*, June 1982, pp. IV-17–IV-28. (Example program on pp. 172–173 was previously published in this paper.)

12

ASSURING
ATE SOFTWARE
RELIABILITY

Errors occur in software as much as in anything else humans do. Once we admit to ourselves that we do make errors, and make them often, we can get on with the task of eliminating them from the things we create. We humans regard errors almost as personal failures and react to them as though they were the product of an inhuman act. Many programmers make their effort to eliminate errors a personal crusade, as though any errors reflected on their basic human abilities. Errors wound the human ego because they prove to us that our work is imperfect. We often respond to an error with a wasteful search for all errors, even the most trivial. Such actions mask the reason for the creation of software, which is to test a UUT, rather than to stand as a monument to an error-free career.

As a result, we should try to work past the human weaknesses with which we have been endowed and approach the task of software reliability in a logical manner. One would hope to produce software that tests the UUT without any errors. The emphasis should be, however, on testing the UUT without significant error, rather than on eliminating all errors, no matter how trivial.

SOFTWARE DESIGN

The best way to end up with software that tests the UUT without error, of course, is to produce perfect software in the first place. Years ago, the U.S. Air Force sponsored a Zero Defects program in which it urged its personnel to try to work without errors. This program had some positive effects on quality and a similar emphasis could bear results in software quality. If an organization could produce error-free software, it would save an enormous amount of debugging and testing expense. According to some estimates, as

Software error costs

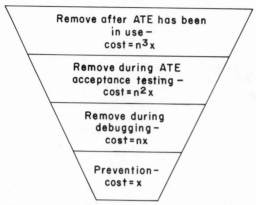

Fig. 12-1 The cost of locating and removing software errors increases manyfold at each later stage of the production process. Preventing the error beforehand is relatively inexpensive. Errors that surface after the software has been in use could be the most expensive. In some cases, the product may have to be recalled.

much as 50 percent of program development budgets goes into software testing.

Although one can seldom produce error-free software for the first time through, the emphasis on error avoidance is still worth the effort. As Fig. 12-1 illustrates, the cost of finding and correcting errors increases manyfold at each stage of the software production process. Similar illustrations appear in numerous texts and articles on software, but one may forget the relative costs of software errors if the subject goes unmentioned. The cost of avoiding an error in the initial stages of design and coding runs less than ridding the software of that error later in the process.

ERROR AVOIDANCE

A number of techniques exist to help the programmer avoid errors. One method that has been popular for some time is the concept called structured programming. Myers defines structured programming as the attitude of writing code with the intent of communicating with people instead of machines.

With this technique, one writes the program in an organized flow to keep it as easy to understand as possible. It is hoped that programmers will introduce fewer errors into their programs if they keep things simple. They will have to juggle fewer program paths if they avoide GOTO statements, for example, and provide only one entrance and exit point in each program module.

The indented format of some programs also makes them easier to follow. Such a program structure helps one to avoid errors and to pick them out more readily during debugging.

COMMENTS, VARIABLES, AND LABELS

Programmers must include meaningful comments in their program to provide guidance during debugging. The emphasis here lies on the word *meaningful,* in the sense that quality is preferred over quantity. Programmers sometimes clutter their programs with confusing or unnecessary comments. Some programmers have developed the ability to sum up in a few words what the program does at that point. A meaningful comment serves as a guidepost to others who must understand the program later. The programmer should also insert comments at the beginning of each program, file, and subroutine to identify it and explain its use and requirements.

Programmers should also select meaningful names for program variables. The use of the variable F seems appropriate for a frequency measurement, but it would confuse others if it represented a voltage measurement. To avoid errors, programmers should also select abbreviations with care. The use of the variable Err as an error flag was discussed in the last chapter. The abbreviation easily became Er during coding. The programmer in this instance should have used the variable $Error$ as the error flag.

Software labels should also have meaningful names. (Note how often the adjective meaningful occurs in this discussion.) The label $DMMSCAN$ indicates that the associated routine has something to do with a DMM and a scanner. Such meaningful labels serve the same purpose as meaningful comments and variables.

The following routine illustrates the importance of meaningful comments and labels. The label in line 0 indicates that the routine will test an amplifier in accordance with paragraph 4.2.1 of the test requirement specification. The inclusion of the TRS paragraph in the label serves as an excellent reference back to the TRS. The comments in lines 1, 4, and 7 clearly show what the following steps will accomplish. The subroutines "CONNECT DVM", "DVM MEASURE" and "OUTOFTOL" that the routine calls are examples of meaningful labels.

```
0:  "4.2.1 AMPLIFIER TESTS":
1:  "READ INPUT VOLTS":
2:  cll 'CONNECT DVM'(36,10)
3:  cll 'DVM MEASURE'(X)
4:  "READ OUTPUT VOLTS":
```

```
5: cll'CONNECT DVM'(24,10)
6: cll'DVM MEASURE'(Z)
7: "CALC GAIN = Z/X":
8: Z/X→G
9: if G⟩15 or G⟨13;gto "OUTOFTOL"
10:prt "PASS, GAIN = ",G
11:ret
12:"OUTOFTOL":
13:prt "FAIL, GAIN = ",G
```

The following routine illustrates the opposite situation. The label in line 0 says nothing about the purpose of the subroutine that is called. It may well refer to the names of the programmers, but one cannot even be sure of that unless the programmers' identities are known. The labels for the subroutines called in lines 1 and 5 also mean nothing. The routine lacks the comments that could guide others through the routine.

```
0: cll'RAYPAC'(36,10)
1: cll 'INOUT' (X)
2: cll 'RAYPAC'(24,10)
3: cll 'INOUT'(Z)
4: Z/X→Y
5: if Y⟩15 or Y⟨13; gto "OUT"
6: prt "PASS"
7: ret
8: "OUT":
9: prt"FAIL"
```

DOCUMENTATION ERRORS

Among the errors that find their way into a program are those that many programmers insist are the total responsibility of others. These errors occur in such documents as the TRS for the UUT. Since programmers refer to them when they write the program, any errors there will cause corresponding errors in the test program. The following are examples of such errors.

1. Errors in the TRS and other documents: The design engineers may introduce these errors before they turn the documents over to the programmers. They may insert an erroneous value, miss a critical test, leave out a section while transcribing the requirements, or fail to catch typographical errors during a review of the document.

2. Errors in the interpretation of the TRS and other documents: The design engineer may write misleading text and the programmer may misinter-

Fig. 12-2 Adequate and correct documentation will help prevent software errors.

pret what was written. The design engineer may delegate the writing of the TRS to an assistant who lacks the experience to understand the UUT, the writing of a TRS, and the testing requirements of UUTs. The programmer may lack the specific experience and training on the UUT to interpret the TRS as intended.

Preventing Documentation Errors

The software group cannot shuck responsibility for the presence of such errors, since it can help prevent them. Rather than assume a defensive attitude and be quick to blame others, the software group should help uncover such errors whenever possible. The software group cannot assume total responsibility for those errors, of course. In their efforts to understand the ATE system and UUT well enough to write the test program, however, they can watch for discrepancies and errors and point them out. This will avoid troublesome errors in the final test program, which the software group will have to take the time to correct anyway. The correction process can introduce other errors, which will cause still more problems in the future.

In a more efficient alternative, the software group helps the UUT group avoid errors in the first place. The programmers will have to work closely with the designers (of hardware and software) in order to learn the UUT well enough to avoid errors and write a good program. This spirit of cooperation will serve the interests of both the individual and the organization in the long run.

The software group can help assure that the final software is free of documentation errors by sponsoring a limited software design review with the UUT designers. The programmer should limit attendees to the UUT designers and those involved from the ATE software group.

At the review, software personnel can discuss the software and present their interpretation of the TRS and other associated documents. They should restrict the presentation to the pertinent points of the TRS and avoid discussions of irrelevant details. The programmer should mention the critical specifications by name and value to assure that they sound reasonable to the UUT designers. It is hoped that they will clarify misconceptions, detect errors, and provide guidance. If an aggressive moderator can keep the review on the topics of interest, errors in the documents that the programmer is using to design the software may be uncovered.

CHECKING CODE

The completed program will contain a number of errors, no matter how much the programmer tries to avoid them. If one accepts the presence of errors and sets out to find those errors, the debugging and testing process will be more productive.

In order to find some errors, one must check the completed code. The programmers can break the program down into modules and step through each line of a module to see that each line is correct and that the module does what it should do. At each input and output statement, they can introduce test cases and step through the code to assure that it handles the test data as it should.

THE WALK-THROUGH

When the programmer is satisfied that the code is correct, other programmers can inspect it for errors. A number of methods exist to accomplish this step. Often, the group gathers in a room and goes through the code step by step. This review and discussion of the code by others can uncover errors that the programmer missed, but the errors found justifies the time involved. This process is educational for all programmers involved, however, because it exposes them to the techniques and style of others.

One popular method of detecting errors is the walk-through, in which the group introduces test cases into the program and walks through the program to see that it produces the correct result. As with the design review covered in a previous chapter, however, the walk-through may be less productive than it could be. The walk-through requires a strong moderator to keep the group on the subject. Otherwise, it will tend to head off toward irrelevant details. Individuals may pair off into unproductive discussions or one individual may tie up the meeting with unimportant details. Some members of a walk-through, as in the design review, may feel challenged to "show their stuff," and they will draw the walk-through in one unproductive direction or another. The walk-through will serve the purpose of uncovering errors only if the moderator keeps it on the subject.

TESTING ATE SOFTWARE

Programmers test their software to uncover errors that will cause the ATE system to pass a defective UUT. Subtle errors can mask UUT defects and programmers must test their software with the intention of finding those errors. They should never run a test with the intention of proving that a program is error-free. Too often, a programmer will try a test case or two, then declare that the software must be error-free because it went through the tests without an error and gave the expected results. Such results may please the programmer, but it will never prove that software is error-free. Small errors can still exist in any one of the hundreds or thousands of lines of an ATE test program. A single error in that program can cause defective UUTs to pass and be placed into service.

Too often the validation and acceptance testing of most ATE software packages consists of running a test or two to show that the software works. The purchaser seldom has enough time to learn the software well enough to evaluate it by the time the ATE system arrives. The manufacturer may give a quick operating course, run a few test cases as part of acceptance testing, then declare that the ATE system and its software are error-free. The organization would be wiser to invest in software training before delivery so the programmers can perform their own evaluation before acceptance tests begin.

The techniques for testing of ATE software will vary with the type of software involved. With a functional test system that is built in-house and dedicated to a particular assembly, the programmer may have to check 5000 lines of code. An ATE system that comes with a test program preparation package may require "programmers" who are typists and test engineers for evaluation. In such a case, the typist will recheck the entered data and the test engineer may match the instructions of the program with the schematic to assure that the program tests all components and interconnections. If the program misses a component, the ATE system will never test it; if that component is misinstalled, missing, or out of tolerance, the ATE system will never indicate a failure and will pass a defective UUT.

A functional, comparison, or system test later may find the defective component, but only if the organization performs such a test and if the test is thorough enough to detect the defect. The intervening circuitry could mask the defect in such tests.

SOFTWARE PACKAGES

Users must ensure that the program they develop from the test program development package is free of the errors that could affect the testing of the UUT. They must ensure that the test program preparation software package itself is also free of defects. An analysis of the package would require answering the following questions:

1. Will a program developed from the package adequately test the UUT as a whole? Will the program apply the stimuli and read the values at all of the test nodes? The user may answer part of this question during the hardware evaluation of the ATE system, which was covered in a previous chapter. The user must also evaluate the rest of the package from a software standpoint.

2. Do the subroutines (such as those in the device library) adequately test the separate parts of the UUT?

When an organization purchases a type of ATE system that has been in use for a number of years, it may expect that the purchase includes debugged and tested software that is free of errors. In fact, a potential purchaser may want to assure that a reputable consulting firm has checked over the software and certified it. An organization should still test the software package, however, to assure that it does what it must do to test the organization's UUTs. The organization must set aside the claims of the salesperson and the brochures and evaluate the software package itself.

A user may believe, for example, that the software will test the devices on a board at "operating speed." A thorough evaluation could uncover the fact that the ATE system will test the components at "operating speed or 1 MHz, whichever is lower." The user may have also had problems with cross talk in a particular UUT when all of the operating signals are applied. An evaluation of the ATE software could reveal that the ATE system can only apply one signal to the UUT at a time, which would prevent the user from applying the multiple signals required to test for the level of cross talk.

A number of methods exist to evaluate the test program preparation software. Some will also check the hardware. The following are a few considerations.

1. Perform a thorough evaluation of the documents and program listings provided with the ATE system. If possible, the user should obtain these documents before delivery or even before purchase. This could be an enormous task, since the software documentation could cover a number of volumes.

2. Write a test program for a UUT, then perform a test with a good UUT

to ensure that the program steps through the test as it should. This test does have limited use in that it fails to uncover those errors that would show up when the ATE system tests a defective UUT. The evaluation with a good UUT will show that the program steps through the test without an obvious error and does serve as a good first step for testing hardware and software. A drawback to this method is that it proves only that the program will test a good UUT. Organizations purchase ATE systems, however, to detect defective UUTs.

3. Perform a test with a UUT into which the tester has introduced a failure. This method will prove that the ATE system and its software together can detect a specific type of failure in a specific UUT component, which is a useful second step. It fails to prove, however, that the software and hardware will detect any other type of failure in any other component. In order to evaluate the ATE thoroughly, then, one would have to expand the method as follows:

   a. The tester must introduce all possible types of defects (misaligned, misinstalled, out-of-tolerance, and defective components) into the UUT and run the test each time. The ATE system should detect each type of fault.
   b. The tester must also install components with each type of defect into each component location and run the test. The ATE system should detect each type of failure in each component location.
   c. The tester must introduce all combinations of defects and components (combinations of defects taken two at a time, then three at a time, etc.) into the UUT and run the test each time. The ATE system should detect all combinations of defects and components and any potential for such time-dependent events as race conditions. The software should provide all test patterns that the UUT will input during operation.

An evaluation of this method will reveal how ridiculous such "thorough" testing can become. Assume that we have a board with only five components and wanted to introduce each type of defect into each component one at a time, then in combination with all of the others. If we group the defects into just three groups—defective (open, short, missing, or out of tolerance), misinstalled (assumed here to be the same as missing), and misoriented— we have a total of 15 different ways that five components could exhibit failures one at a time.

If we consider any two components having a defect of some type at the same time, we would have to add the total combinations of the components taken two at a time. The following indicates the many ways that the defects of two components could combine.

| | COMPONENT | | | | |
Case	1	2	3	4	5
1	0	0	0	1	1
2	.	.	.	1	2
3	.	.	.	1	3
4	.	.	.	2	1
.	.	.	.	2	2

Note: 0 = good; 1 = out of tolerance; 2 = misinstalled; 3 = misoriented

Since a typical board contains dozens of components, a "thorough" evaluation would require an astronomical number of tests. If we consider the testing of an assembly with many boards, the extent of the test becomes even more unreasonable. Note that such tests also check hardware.

Obviously, then, the organization has to settle for less testing. A combination of methods will serve to build up some confidence in the test program preparation package. Since some personnel must study the documents to familiarize themselves with the system, they can be instructed to look for discrepancies and limitations. They can also evaluate any acceptance test the manufacturer will run and any self-test that comes with the ATE system to see if it will test the software. One can also write a program, then run a good UUT to see that the program steps through the test as expected. This step will prove that the software will at least work with the user's unique combination of components in the UUT.

The introduction of defects into the UUT presents a more complicated problem, as has already been seen. Users cannot introduce all types of defects into all component locations. One can use fault simulation software supplied by the manufacturer to evaluate test programs and evaluate their thoroughness. Such software can also contain subtle defects and limitations that can mask program defects.

TEST PRIORITIES

Because of the enormous number of tests that one would have to run to evaluate any test program thoroughly, the user must set priorities on the testing of software.

1. The portions of the software that would test the most critical UUT specifications should have the highest priority for testing. If an ICT will test a board on which a decoder and some gates will test a critical UUT signal, one would test that type of decoder and IC in order of their importance

to final product quality. The software department may find such lists difficult to obtain from the UUT designers unless it indicates that it requires the information to improve the testing of the UUTs.

2. The software that tests sections of the UUT that one knows are prone to failure should also have a high priority for testing. If possible, the evaluator should insert the same type of defects (or simulate the defects) that occur in the components of the circuits involved. If a particular decoder chip on a certain board is often misinstalled, for example, one should misinstall the component. In order to determine the failure-prone components, the evaluator will have to search repair records and interview technicians who have previously performed troubleshooting on that UUT on the bench or a manual test set.

TESTING USER-GENERATED SOFTWARE

The organization that creates its own software will face problems different from those that the user of prepared software faces. The user who generates ATE software will experience many of the same problems as programmers who create software for other purposes, such as circuit design or modeling. A number of techniques exist to test software. The following is a brief description of some techniques.

1. *Bottom-up testing:* With this technique, the programmer begins the test at the lowest module, then continues in steps up to the top modules. The programmer first tests the lowermost modules that perform without any inputs. If they pass, one can assume they are reliable and higher-level modules can use them through a CALL or GOSUB command. With a base of tested modules, the programmer can continue to the next level and test those higher-level modules using the previously tested modules, and so on to the topmost modules. This process continues until all of the modules from the bottom to the top have been tested. The programmer must use a portion of software called a *module driver* in order to input test cases to each module.

2. *Top-down testing:* With this technique, the programmer tests the modules from the highest to the lowest levels. Before the actual testing can begin, the programmer must first perform some initial work to make the input, output, and other such modules operational. Software *stub modules* are required to simulate the lower-level modules (as yet nonexistent or untested) that the higher-level modules will call. Stub modules provide the inputs that the calling module expects.

3. *Sandwich testing:* This method combines the features of both of the previous techniques. With this technique, both bottom-up and top-down

testing begin simultaneously. Sandwich testing is especially useful with large programs.

TEST SIMULATION

An organization that creates its own programs can test those programs in a software laboratory. The programmer can simulate the tests and introduce any number of test cases required to test the software. Such simulation has a number of benefits and allows the programmer to do the following:

1. Test the software under conditions that approximate those of the actual testing conditions.

2. Test the software in a laboratory without interfering with ATE operation.

3. Introduce any desired test case into the software in order to test the response.

A number of texts recommend that the programmer choose enough test cases to test each path in a program. If one speaks of unique paths, such a requirement could be impractical. If a program contains 100 decision points, the testing could require thousands of tests. A more practical course would consist of testing the two decision paths at least once for each of the 100 decision points.

A number of texts also discuss the philosophies of test-case design. At one extreme, the programmer ignores the program itself and designs tests based on the requirements of the specifications. At the other end of the philosophical spectrum, the programmer ignores the specifications and goes into the program to test the code. With ATE software, the programmer should use both to some extent, but the nature of UUT testing probably dictates that we test to the UUT specifications more often.

Selecting Modules for Test

We can develop criteria for selecting modules for test. These criteria are similar to those used to evaluate test-program preparation packages. If time permits, of course, the programmer can test all modules. A program of a few thousand lines, however, would require that the programmer give some modules priority over others. The following are some considerations in selecting the modules for test.

1. The programmer should give the highest priority for testing to the program modules that will test the most critical UUT specifications.

2. The modules susceptible to error should also have a high priority for

testing. If a module has a defect, for example, one may want to test all similar modules to see if they have the same type of defect.

3. Modules that have nothing to do with the actual testing of the UUT assume a low testing priority. Such modules may print out explanatory notes, for example, or provide an impressive CRT display for the operator at the beginning of the test.

Simulation of Test Cases

To test software modules, one can introduce test data into the modules and observe how the module handles that test data. The programmer can perform this testing in the software laboratory or on the ATE by simulating actual test data inputs and outputs.

In order to run the test in a laboratory, the programmer must first eliminate any input-output statements that will cause an error message, then substitute keyboard entry statements. The programmer can then enter any value of test data desired and observe the results. The module must receive enough test cases that the most likely errors show up. As was discussed in the last chapter, arrays, calculations, and pass-fail, READ/DATA, and input-output routines have a high testing priority. The programmer should always test the boundary conditions, just inside and outside specified limits.

Before the testing begins, the programmer must first plan out the testing session. All test data should come from an official document other than the program or its associated documents. This requirement will bring out errors that were introduced during the transcription of the specifications.

The most logical document to use, of course, is the latest copy of the test requirements specifications from the UUT design engineer. By using the latest copy of the TRS, the programmer will check whether the test program includes all of the latest revisions. Another method of checking that the latest TRS version is used is to include its revision number and date as a comment at the beginning of the program. If this method is used, however, one must assure that a procedure has been adopted to update the revision number and date every time the software is changed.

The programmer must next list all of the test cases that will be used and compute the expected results. The software should provide a printout of the results keyed to the list of test cases. One should always plan the test cases beforehand. Some programmers sit at the terminal and enter test cases at random to see what will occur. With this method, one can never be assured of running enough of the correct tests.

The programmer will then load the program module and eliminate all instructions that will give an error, such as GPIB I/O statements. The following is a routine that reads the voltage at a test point, then uses the measured value in some calculations. When the programmer attempts to run the routine on a laboratory desktop computer, the program will attempt to read in a DMM value from the GPIB (line 101), detect that nothing is at the interface, and display an error message. The programmer must replace the statements in line 101 and 102 with those that allow keyboard entry of test values.

```
100: "VOLTFREQ":51→Z
101: red"FRQCTR",F
102: red"DVM",V
103: gsb"POWER"
104: V*F→Y
105: if Y⟩=10260 and Y⟨=12180;gto "PASSY"
106: prt"FAIL: Y=",Y;gto +2
107: "PASSY";prt "PASS: Y=",Y
108: gto"TESTWO"
109: "POWER":V↑2/Z→P
110: if P⟩=14.238 and P⟨=16.426;gto "PASSP"
111: prt "FAIL:P=",P;gto +2
112: "PASSP":prt "PASS: P=",P
113: ret
114: "TESTWO":
```

The following is the same routine modified to allow such keyboard inputs. Lines 102 and 103 now contain ent (enter) statements, which allow the entry of test data directly from the keyboard into the routine. Line 101 allows the programmer to enter a run number, which will print out with the test results. With the run number on the printout, the programmer has a reference back to the test-case list that was prepared beforehand.

```
100: "VOLTFREQ":51→Z
101: ent "ENTER RUN #",R
102: ent "ENTER FREQUENCY",F
103: ent "ENTER VOLT",V
104: prt "RUN#=",R
105: gsb "POWER"
106: V*F→Y
107: if Y⟩=10260 and Y⟨=12180;gto "PASSY"
108  prt "FAIL: Y=",Y;gto 100
109  "PASSY":prt "PASS: Y=",Y;gto 100
111: "POWER":V↑2/Z→P
112: if P⟩=14.238 and P⟨=16.426;gto "PASSP"
113: prt "FAIL: P=",P;gto +2
114: "PASSP":prt "PASS: P=",P
115: ret
116: "TESTWO":
```

The programmer can now run the modified routine in the laboratory and enter any test values whatsoever for voltage and frequency. The routine will use the entered values just as it would if the counter or DMM had provided those values over the GPIB. The programmer can simulate any desired test conditions and observe whether the program provides the correct results. The following is an example of some test data that the programmer could use for V and F. Notice that the values lie just inside and outside the boundary of the specified limits (27 to 29 V for V; 380 to 420 Hz for F).

Run	V	F	Run	V	F
1	26.99	380	5	26.99	379
2	27.01	380	6	26.99	381
3	28.99	420	7	28.99	381
4	29.01	420	8	27.01	379

The following are the results from the first four tests.

```
RUN# = 1.00
PASS: P = 14.28
FAIL: Y = 10256.20
RUN# 2.00
PASS: P = 14.30
PASS: Y = 10263.80
RUN# 3.00
FAIL: P = 16.48
PASS: Y = 12175.80
RUN# 4.00
FAIL: P = 16.50
FAIL: Y = 12184.20
```

Run 1 indicates a PASS. Since V was outside the allowable limits, however, the test should have failed. The software obviously contains an error. An analysis of documents that were generated early in the project would have revealed that the resistance in line 100 should have been 51.2 Ω. The design engineer accidentally rounded off the load resistance value before sending it to the programmer. The programmer would have never uncovered this error if the test case values had been farther from the boundary values.

Errors could still exist in the portion inside the specified limits, but this would be less likely than the existence of errors near the boundary conditions. As is often said in testing, one would rather fail good UUTs than pass defective ones, and the routine would fail good UUTs if an error exists within the specified limits. Although this philosophy has some limitations, in that one wants to avoid the waste of technician's time chasing failures in good UUTs, it does support the use of more test cases near the boundary and into the fail region.

The programmer can also use the simulation technique to test routines that provide circuit stimulus. A routine similar to the one discussed in a previous chapter is shown below. It provides a square wave swept in frequency from 3 to 99 kHz. One may want to refer back for an explanation on how the routine works.

```
425 Swpout: ! Waveform Sweep
435 DIM Freq (6)
445 RESTORE 615
455 A$ = "+100M1K"
465 OUTPUT 701;"C+4KB1KF3000E+3KA0200E0KD"&A$!Init Frq = 3
475 CALL Mux (2,"3")
485 READ Freq (*) ! Begin Sweep
495 Lofrq = Freq (4)
505 FOR Loop = 1 TO 7
515 Lofrq = Lofrq + 1000
525 OUTPUT 701;"F"&VAL$(Lofrq)&"E+3K"! 3 – 9 KHz Sweep
535 NEXT Loop
545 Medfrq = Freq(6)
555 FOR Loop = 1 TO 91
565 Medfrq = Medfrq + 100
575 OUTPUT 701;"F"&VAL$(Medfrq)&"E+4K"! 10 – 99 KHz Sweep
585 NEXT Loop
595 ! END Sweep; Disconnect Waveform Gen
605 OUTPUT 718;"DS"
615 DATA 1132,.608,8.977,2000,5000,900,900
625 RETURN
```

The following routine has been modified to allow its testing in the software laboratory. Lines in the routine that the programmer changed have been appended with -SIM to make the new steps easy to locate. A DISP (Display) statement has replaced the OUTPUT statements in lines 465, 525, and 595. The programmer has also introduced WAIT 500 statements to slow down the steps in frequency. The WAIT 500 statement in line 535 will stop the incrementation of frequency in the first loop for 500 ms, long enough for the programmer to observe the latest step. The statement in line 605 will stop the frequency in the second loop, but only for a few values at the beginning and end of the loop.

```
425 Swpout: ! Waveform Sweep
435 DIM Freq(6)
```

```
445 RESTORE 645
455 A$ = "+100M1K"
465 DISP701;"C+4KB1KF3000E+3KA0200E0KD"&A$!InitFreq=3  −SIM
475 ! CALL Mux (2,"3")  −SIM
485 READ Freq (*)! Begin Sweep
495 Lofrq = Freq(4)
505 FOR Loop = 1 TO 7
515 Lofrq = Lofrq + 1000
525 DISP 701;"F"&VAL$(Lofrq)&"E+3K"! 3−9 kHz Sweep  −SIM
535 WAIT 500! − SIM
545 NEXT Loop
555 PAUSE ! − SIM
565 Medfrq = Freq (6)
575 FOR Loop = 1 TO 91
585 Medfrq = Medfrq + 100
595 DISP 701;"F"&VAL$(Medfrq)&"E+4K"! 10−99 kHz Sweep  −SIM
605 IF (Loop ⟨7) OR (Loop⟩85) THEN WAIT 300! − SIM
615 NEXT Loop
625 ! End Sweep; Disconnect Waveform Gen
635:! OUTPUT 718;"DS"  −SIM
645 DATA 1132,.608,8.977,2000,5000,900,900
655 GOTO 425! − SIM
```

The test should uncover a number of errors. The tester will see that the first loop starts to increment the frequency from 6 kHz instead of 3 kHz. The programmer made an error in the calling of the initial data in line 495 and called 5000 instead of 2000 as an input value to the first loop. The tester will also observe that the program steps up to 100 kHz instead of 99 kHz because of the value of Loop in line 575. Another error in line 455 could cause the dc offset voltage to assume the wrong value. The string value of A$ should have been "+100KM1K" instead of "+100M1K," but the tester would probably have overlooked this error because of the focus on the incrementation of frequency. (This example appeared in the *Proceedings of the ATE Seminar/Exhibit,* June 1982.)

DEBUGGING

If the software indicates during testing or operation that it contains an error, the programmer must locate and correct the error. Such debugging of ATE software follows much the same process as does the debugging of other types of software. The intimate relationship between hardware and software in ATE does dictate, however, that the programmer become involved in the complexities of hardware (and the hardware design engineer will become involved to some degree with the software).

As a first step in the process, of course, the programmer must locate the error. An analysis of the test cases and results will often indicate the most logical area in which to try first to locate the error. If a program consists of five major sections, for example, and an error results only in the last section, the programmer would go first to that section.

The fallacy behind the standard methods of debugging is that they detect and eliminate only the most obvious of errors. This step is a necessary one, of course, since it will eliminate those errors. Too often, however, the programmer will eliminate those obvious errors, then judge the program to be error-free. The program will probably never be error-free, so one should set the goal of correcting all the errors possible that affect the testing of the UUT and reflect on final product quality.

During initial debugging, many obvious errors will show up without the need for many test cases. The programmer could easily overlook even an obvious error, however, unless each result is analyzed carefully. The following test-result printout illustrates such an example.

2.1.1 VOLTS COMPARISON
EXPECTED VALUE: 2.732 − 2.818
MEASURED VALUE: 2.881
PASS

The programmer could miss the error in this printout if it received a cursory analysis. A programmer who is fatigued from the day's work and schedule pressures may accept the pass printout as an indication that the program itself has passed the test. Since the measured value lies outside of the expected limits, however, an error must exist in the software. The following could cause such an error:

1. The expected value on the printout may be incorrect. Suppose that the limits should be 2.732 to 2.918. In this instance, the program may test for the correct limits but provide an incorrect printout with an error in the upper limit. In this instance, the ATE system will never pass bad UUTs. The programmer should still check the actual upper and lower limits and associated statements for correctness, however, since the presence of one error may indicate that other errors exist. The programmer could well say "I found the error!" and be lulled into overlooking additional errors that exist.

2. The printout is correct but the program uses incorrect values for the limits.

This error is more serious. The following illustrates a routine with errors that could cause such a situation:

```
35 prt"EXPECTED VALUE: 2.732 − 2.818"
36 prt "MEASURED VALUE: ",V
37 if V⟩=2.732 and V⟨= 2.918; prt "PASS";gto +2
38 prt "FAIL"
```

The routine contains an error in that it tests for an upper limit in line 37 of 2.918 instead of the correct value of 2.818 printed in line 35. (Of course, we could also use this routine to illustrate the situation in the previous case where the printout is in error. In this instance, an error would exist in line 35 rather than line 37.)

A more difficult situation would exist if the program contained two errors. If the expected value and the value in the limits were incorrect, the programmer may correct one and fail to check for the other.

Unfortunately, the programmer may seldom have the fortune to write programs that contain only obvious errors, as in the above example. Too often, a number of questionable steps combine to constitute a subtle error. The following is an example of such an error:

```
25 wrt "DVM", "ACVOLTS"
26 red "DVM", V
27 if V⟩=27.5 and V =⟨28.5;prt"PASS"
    .
    .
    .

176 wrt "DVM","ACVOLTS"
177 red "DVM",A
    .
    .
    .

192 if V⟩=27.5 and V =⟨28.5;prt"PASS"
    .
    .
    .
```

In line 26, the program measures a voltage at a test point and assigns the measured value to the variable V. Later, another voltage in the same range is measured at the same test point. The program assigns this value to the variable A. After some computations, the programmer tests for the value of V instead of A in line 192. Since the program has assigned the value of a previous measurement to this variable, the program will check that value again, instead of the value assigned to A in step 177. As a result, the program checks the value measured in line 27. Since the variable V suits a voltage measurement better than A, one could easily commit this error. Perhaps the programmer stopped for the day at some point between lines 177 and 192, then mixed up the variables after resuming work the next day.

CORRECTING THE ERROR

One writer estimates that as many as 50 percent of the changes made in a program to correct errors result in new errors. The following are some ways the programmer can insert new errors:

1. The programmer corrects the symptoms rather than the cause. In the example above where the program contained erroneous specifications, the programmer could solve the problem by changing the specifications to conform to the printout. If the printout contains the error, however, the programmer would introduce a more serious error.

2. The programmer erroneously changes lines while making the correction. A common error occurs when the programmer deletes an adjacent line in the process of making a correction. The programmer could also write over a line while storing the new line. One calculator allows the programmer to insert a line between two other lines in the program or to store a new line over the old one. If one presses Store instead of Insert, one program line would be deleted.

3. The programmer makes an error in the new lines. This can result from an error during keyboard entry, an error in the code itself, or an error in the new algorithm. The latter can be the most subtle and difficult to detect in later debugging runs. If the error resulted because the programmer misunderstood an instruction (something easy to do if the programmer seldom uses that instruction), the same error could exist in other places in the program.

4. The programmer inserts experimental statements "to see what will happen," then inadvertently leaves them in the program. The programmer must document such insertions, then be sure that they are deleted.

EFFECTIVE DEBUGGING

A number of methods exist for improving the results of debugging. Programmers themselves can take a number of obvious steps, such as making an effort to understand the language and each instruction that is used in the program. They can also remain alert to the possibility that they can overlook subtle errors or introduce them when they are correcting errors. The following are some suggestions to make debugging more effective.

1. The programmer can use available debugging tools. A debugging tool may allow the programmer to set breakpoints, for example, and go into the program and make changes to see the effects during operation. Some computers have a trace mode that prints out intermediate results.

2. After the programmer has made corrections, the new listing should be compared to the old listing in the changed areas. The programmer should walk through the segment from a few statements before the change to a few statements after the change to ensure that the inserted statements will perform as expected. One should look for changed or deleted lines.

3. After the corrections, the programmer should repeat the tests that indicated the errors in the first place. All test data should be rerun to ensure that the new segment performs as expected. Too often, the programmer ensures only that the new segments work and fail to test each segment enough to be certain that all errors have been eliminated.

4. The programmer should maintain a master copy of the latest version of the program on a convenient storage medium. This master copy includes all the latest changes. A working version can be used to experiment with program changes. The programmer should delete these changes as soon as their usefulness ends, since they could mask errors that exist in the master copy if they remain. As much as possible, the programmer should test and debug with a working version that is a copy of the master program. Before and after the programmer inserts changes in the master copy, however, they must be reviewed and tested.

DEBUGGING HARDWARE AND SOFTWARE

At some point in the process, the programmer will take the software to the ATE system and test and debug it on the hardware. This mating of hardware and software creates a potential for errors unlike that which may exist in a "soft" system in which the computer performs all calculations and outputs without interfacing with the hardware (except for peripherals). With computer-aided design, for example, the design engineer designs the circuitry entirely on a CRT display and may never see the hardware.

With ATE that is built in-house, hardware engineers and programmers may debug the hardware and software simultaneously. This situation contains an even greater potential for error. One reason for this is that hardware complexities and errors can mask software errors. The programmer must become familiar enough with the hardware to work with the hardware engineer in the debugging of both hardware and software. The programmer can gain confidence in the software only if error-free hardware exists on which to debug it.

As a result, the hardware designer and the programmer should generally concentrate on debugging the hardware first, although some software debugging must take place simultaneously. The programmer can design software tests that can uncover hardware errors. The programmer should also insist that they run enough tests with a variety of parameters to ensure that the hardware performs as it should. If the programmer has developed a self-test program for the hardware, it will have to be debugged before being used to check the hardware.

After the debugging of the hardware, the emphasis will shift to the software. This shift of emphasis takes place when all of the necessary tests have been run and the incidence of detected errors has tapered off to the point where further tests would be unproductive. (During the software tests, however, numerous hardware errors can still crop up, and usually do.)

During the next phase, the programmer may run the UUT test program with a UUT to assure that the program tests the UUT as expected. The programmer must ensure that hardware complexities or errors cannot mask a corresponding software error. The programmer should have worked closely with the hardware design engineer in order to have enough knowledge of the hardware to spot potential sources of error. On the other hand, the hardware design engineer should be aware what outputs each portion of software provides to the hardware and what values it expects to read in. The two can then discuss any points of potential conflict or errors that could be masked.

Too often, the hardware and software designers want only to prove that the ATE system will test UUTs. Although both may harbor fears that a subtle error may someday emerge and be shown to have caused a problem in product quality, they too often direct their efforts only toward getting the ATE to run a test on a good UUT.

During the initial design stages, they may have rechecked all their work to avoid any errors. After the ATE system is built and on the floor for testing, however, they may experience a self-inflicted pressure to get the ATE hardware and software checked out as quickly as possible. They may consider the errors that crop up during testing and debugging to be minor, whereas they would have considered them major if they had occurred during a previous stage. The programmer, for example, might experience pangs of self-doubt and anxiety over such an obvious error during coding. On the test floor, however, the emphasis rests on "getting the thing working" and changes are made "on the fly" to patch over what could potentially be a major error or a series of errors.

USING THE ATE TO TEST SOFTWARE

The hardware engineer and programmer can use the ATE itself to test the software. The programmer can place a PAUSE at each point in the UUT test program where the system makes a measurement, then run the program and simulate the input values. Suppose the program connects a UUT connector pin to the frequency counter to measure the signal frequency at that point. The hardware engineer can connect a signal generator to the ATE input to simulate the UUT signal, continue with the program, then check the printout to see that the measured value is correct.

This method can consume some time and be difficult to implement, since the program would require stimuli for all UUT inputs. To perform the test correctly, of course, the programmer should loop on the test and input a range of values, especially around the boundary conditions.

Another method utilizes the UUT itself. The programmer connects the UUT, then runs the test program in which the PAUSE statements were inserted. Each time the program pauses, the programmer can measure the UUT test point, then continue with the program. The programmer can compare the measured value with the value on the printout to assure that they compare.

The disadvantage of this method, of course, is that it tests the software for only one value in each test. The programmer cannot vary the value at the point to test the boundary conditions. As a result, this method is useful for initial testing, but it cannot be considered an extensive software test.

SOFTWARE RELIABILITY

Since errors can always remain in a program, one should realize that software reliability is an elusive quality. An organization should see to it that its software is properly documented and that a copy of the latest revision and a history of all changes is maintained in a central location. The software group should maintain a programmer's file for each project, with relevant notes, flowcharts, and a listing annotated with the programmer's additional comments. Any person in the future who has doubts about a program will find the information useful to investigate the possibility of an error without having to check the program step by step.

REFERENCES

Bateman, Vernon W.: "Software Quality—Key to Productivity," *36th Annual Quality Congress Transactions*, 1982, pp. 767–770.

D'Angelo, Phil: "Good Software Depends on Proper Testing and Management," *Electronic Design*, Oct. 29, 1981, pp. 187–190.

———: "Structured Analysis Simplifies Modern Software Design," *Electronic Design*, Sept. 3, 1981, pp. 159–168.

Myers, Glenford J.: *Software Reliability*, Wiley (New York), 1976.

Software Tool Catalog, Report No. OSD/FCTC-82/013, Federal Software Testing Center, Falls Church, Va., Apr. 1982.

A Software Tools Project: A Means of Capturing Technology and Improving Engineering, Report No. OSD-82-101, Federal Software Testing Center, Falls Church, Va., Feb. 1982.

Stover, Allan C.: "ATE Software Inspection," *Quality,* Dec. 1981, pp. 26–27.

————: "Can ATE be Trusted by QC?" *Electronic Packaging and Production,* Oct. 1981, pp. 140–144, and *Electronic Production* (United Kingdom), Jan. 1982, pp. 17–21.

————: "How to Improve the Quality of Programs," *Canadian Datasystems,* Aug. 1981, pp. 60–61.

————: "Quality Problems with Automatic Test Equipment," *36th Annual Quality Congress Transactions,* 1982, pp. 771–776.

————: "Software Simulation Techniques Improve ATE Quality," *Proceedings of ATE Seminar/Exhibit,* June 1982, pp. IV-17–IV-28.

Urdaneta, Nelson, Christopher Chui, and John Robinson: "Structured Programming Cuts GPIB Software Costs," *Electronic Design,* Feb. 4, 1982.

13

ATE FAULT LOCALIZATION

Subtle faults can be introduced into ATE hardware or software during design or development. Part failures can also occur during operation. Examples of such faults include software errors, miswiring, parts failures, and design errors. Unless such faults are detected, located, and eliminated, they can cause a stoppage in production or a subtle degradation of product quality.

Much of the delay in locating ATE faults results from the unsatisfactory approach that ATE personnel take when they become involved. Such an approach often results because of either a lack of experience on the specific ATE system or the use of undesirable methods. The aptly-named "shotgun" approach is an example of an undesirable method, where one pursues random causes as they come to mind.

With another common approach, often caused by a lack of familiarity with the defective ATE, one relies too heavily on the advice of other personnel, such as operators whose experience is limited to ATE operation or faults in the UUT. Such personnel are often deceptively familiar with ATE operation, but may be unqualified to locate subtle ATE hardware or software faults. They can give valuable information on the idiosyncracies of the ATE system, however, and should be questioned.

The lack of a systematic approach to locating ATE faults often results in a waste of technical worker-hours and the loss of the ATE system from the production line. The following is one step-by-step approach to ATE fault localization.

1. Define the problem.

2. Determine whether the fault lies in hardware or software.

3. Narrow down the fault to the lowest level necessary.

4. Assure that all faults are eliminated.

Such a systematic approach allows one to take action quickly instead of wasting time on an unorganized approach to the problem.

DEFINING THE PROBLEM

The first task upon learning that a problem exists is to gather preliminary information. The object at this point should be to learn the nature of the suspected fault and the symptoms in order to define the problem. Once the problem itself is defined, one can proceed systematically toward a solution.

One can question the operator and test engineer in order to define as precisely as possible the problem that precipitated the original complaint. A symptom described as "It doesn't work right" must be pursued until one can define it better. A symptom such as "The voltage at the test point is out of specification but the printout says pass" is precise enough to proceed on to the next step. An inquiry should also be made as to whether anyone has performed modifications or software changes recently or a similar problem has occurred in the past. One can also determine any idiosyncracies of the ATE, as well as the UUT requirements for the tests that fail.

HARDWARE OR SOFTWARE?

In the next step, one must determine whether the fault lies in hardware or software. ATE personnel need to spend only enough time to determine with a *reasonable* certainty whether the fault lies in hardware or software. The goal at this point should be to raise the probability of selecting the correct one to its highest level in a reasonable time. Although one will occasionally be in error and have to start over again, the average time to locate faults in ATE will be reduced if a reasonable determination is made at this point.

Two ways exist to determine whether ATE hardware or software contains the fault.

1. Prove that one of the two is the probable cause.

2. Eliminate one of the two as the probable cause.

One can thus perform tests and analyses with the thought of accomplishing either of the two.

In the above effort one can use a number of aids.

1. An analysis of the symptoms themselves will often indicate whether hardware or software is the most probable cause. If the problem has just occurred, for example, the fault is unlikely to be in the test program unless it was recently modified.

2. Information gathered so far on past repairs, calibrations, and modifications may point toward the cause.

3. If an ATE self-test program exists, it can be run to determine whether a hardware or test equipment fault exists. If so, the program may even indicate the location of the fault. Such programs often check only a fraction of the hardware, however, and a pass indication will seldom indicate with certainty that the hardware is free of faults.

4. Additional tests can be devised to ensure that the test equipment performs properly and that continuity exists along the critical signal paths. Use of the ATE controller may speed up such tests.

5. Sections of software that could cause the problem can be tested with standard software checking techniques. Test equipment can also be set up to send testing signals back to the controller. Certain parts of suspected software can be tested with I/O simulation techniques, which were covered in a previous chapter.

If none of the methods provides a definite indication of where the fault lies, one will have to select either hardware or software as the cause of the problem. The information and test results obtained so far will have to be weighed, and a judgment will have to be made as to which of the two most of the evidence points toward.

NARROWING DOWN THE FAULT

Once a decision has been made as to whether the fault lies in hardware or software, one should utilize testing techniques to narrow down the fault to the lowest level for which one has responsibility. In some organizations, for example, the responsibility for software passes to another group. In such a situation, one must simply prove that the fault lies in software. In other organizations, the support engineer must correct both the hardware and software. When the fault has been proved to be in a particular item of test equipment, the responsibility for the repair of that instrument may pass to a calibration laboratory.

In the effort to narrow down the fault, one should utilize information gathered up to this point to determine which section of hardware or software is most likely to cause the problem. An analysis of the symptoms is especially useful. One should then concentrate all efforts on the suspected section until the fault is either located or determined to lie elsewhere. In the latter case, one will have to start over and determine the next most likely location of the fault. Since numerous standard techniques exist to troubleshoot hardware and software, they will not be covered here in detail.

Hardware Fault Localization

The ATE controller can be programmed to test many portions of the hardware. One can write short routines on the spot to test suspected areas. If the ATE self-test program has not yet been run, it can be used to check portions of the hardware and test equipment.

Standard troubleshooting techniques, which utilize such test equipment as oscilloscopes and multimeters, can also be used to locate the fault. One can trace signals, check voltages, compare signatures, and test for continuity in the effort to narrow down the problem.

The half-splitting technique is also useful here. One can begin halfway through the suspected circuit and make the necessary measurements. If the voltages and signals are correct at this point, one next checks a point halfway between there and the input. This division continues until one locates the fault.

Software Error Localization

Standard techniques can be used to locate a software fault. One can check the code, for example, and walk through the suspected routines in order to determine the correctness of each instruction. An especially useful technique is I/O simulation, in which input statements are replaced with statements that allow entry of variables from the controller keyboard. Output statements that provide values to test equipment are changed to display statements. One can thus simulate inputs and observe how the program handles the values. The sequence of output values can also be displayed to determine whether a fault exists there.

One can also single step through the suspected section of the program and observe the reaction of the test equipment and hardware at each point. A Trace mode can often be used, depending on the capabilities of the controller, and the values that are printed out can be analyzed to determine the possible location of the fault.

At some point, one will isolate the fault to a section of the hardware or software that now becomes the responsibility of others to correct. In some organizations, policy or union rules often determine how far down the engineer can go. If the fault is known to exist in a certain circuit, for example, a technician may take over and determine which of a dozen or so parts in the circuit is defective. Before the ATE is turned over, one should consider performing additional tests as time permits if necessary to further support the conclusion of where the fault exists.

GPIB FAULTS

One will sometimes narrow a problem down to the GPIB. A device on the bus could malfunction, for example, and affect the operation of the other devices. It may develop a short circuit to ground on one of the data lines, so that data line will always be at 0. Any commands or data on the bus that require that line to be at a logical 1 will be in error.

Most often, however, the problems on the GPIB are software-related. The ATE designers plug in everything and try to run the self-test program or the test program itself, but the ATE system fails to operate as it should. The programmer could have made an error in the program, for example, so the controller places incorrect commands on the GPIB. The programmer could also have selected the wrong address for a device.

A more common software problem results from an incorrect message format to the devices. There are a number of possibilities:

1. The programmer misunderstood the format requirements that the device manufacturer gave in the operating manual. The sequence can be complicated and one can easily make an error. A generator, for example, could require a string such as the following for it to be set up:

    "Z + 5KB4KF8000E + 2KQ0200KD + 100KM1K"

    Each element between the letter K in the string signifies a different setup parameter. One element specifies the type of waveform, another amplitude, another frequency, another offset, and so on. The term "F8000E + 2" sets the frequency and everything after "D" at the end sets the offset. One will select each element from a number of lists of device parameters. How a device will react to an incorrect parameter depends on the device itself and what parameter it does receive. It could operate, but give an incorrect or default value for that parameter, or it could fail to operate at all.

2. The programmer could make an error while coding the message format. As the string for the generator in the above example shows, an error is easy to make, considering the number of unrelated digits and characters that one must string together in just the right way.

3. The programmer codes the correct format but the controller sends something other than what is expected. The manufacturer may document these idiosyncracies, or may neglect to mention them because they seem obvious or might reflect unfavorably on the controller itself. One could program the controller to send out + 0.038, for example, since the device must receive that value to operate correctly. The controller, on the other hand, could convert all values less than 1 to scientific notation and send out 3.8E-2 instead. If the device cannot handle this value, it will malfunction in some way. Some controllers send extra characters before or after a transmission, such as a line feed or carriage return. The controller and device formats may therefore be incompatible.

GPIB Analyzer

A GPIB, or bus, analyzer allows one to monitor activity on the bus. It generally plugs into the bus with a standard cable as all other devices on the bus. Although bus analyzers vary in their capabilities, most allow monitoring of the data lines and some of the command lines of the GPIB. Many also have capabilities found in logic analyzers, such as data storage and triggering.

Fig. 13-1 shows the Racal-Dana 488 GPIB Analyzer. Since it is small and battery-operated, it can be used in difficult environments. Its LCD monitor displays the status of the data lines (in hexadecimal format) as well as the ATN, SRQ, EOI, DAV, IFC, REN, NRFD, and NDAC lines. Its local RAM storage allows storage and displays of up to 40 samples of the data, ATN, SRQ, and EOI lines, one at a time.

The 488 also allows one to establish a trigger condition for a particular data word and ATN, SRQ, and EOI lines. Only when that particular trigger condition appears on the bus will the 488 activate. One can choose to capture data before, during, or after the trigger, and thus look at 40 words after or before the trigger or 20 words on each side of it.

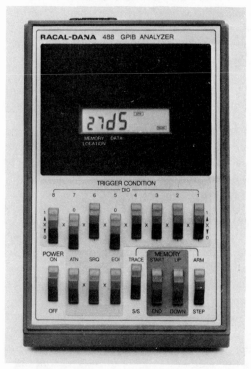

Fig. 13-1 Racal-Dana 488 GPIB Analyzer. *(Courtesy of Racal-Dana Instruments, Inc.)*

The 488 operates in three modes:

Passive, which displays bus activity as it occurs

Trace, which provides memory storage

Single step, in which one can stop on a trigger condition and then single-step through the program

One can thus monitor bus activity as it relates to a particular device on the bus by setting the address of that device and related bus conditions as a trigger. The analyzer will show erroneous commands and message formats and allow one to determine the cause of the problems. One can take corrective action, then recheck bus activity to be certain that the error was corrected and to check whether additional errors were introduced.

ELIMINATING THE FAULTS

Even though other personnel may take on the task of eliminating the fault, the support engineer probably still retains the following responsibility:

1. Ensuring that the fault has been eliminated

2. Ensuring that additional faults have not been introduced. It would be possible, for example, for a technician to damage a sensitive integrated circuit when a resistor is soldered into place nearby. Programmers can also introduce additional faults when they change the program to eliminate the original fault.

Before turning over the responsibility for eliminating the fault, one should analyze the circuit or program and note where faults can most easily be introduced. When things are turned over to other personnel, one can mention the possibility of additional faults in certain areas and advise caution.

After the fault has supposedly been eliminated, one must determine what action was taken, then prove that the fault has been eliminated. This is often an uncomplicated matter in that the tests that were performed to locate the fault can now be repeated to verify that the fault was eliminated. One should then run additional tests to ensure that other faults were not introduced. If a circuit component was replaced, for example, tests should be run on adjacent circuits to check for damage. If software has been changed, one should check the new code, step through it, and observe that it performs as it should. If the new code is a subroutine that other portions of the program call, its effect on other sections should be determined. One should also check whether adjacent instructions have been inadvertently changed or deleted.

If one suspects additional hardware or software defects, it is usually advisable to request an explanation from those who were involved in the corrective action. It would be possible, for example, that they performed a modification in the course of correcting the original defect. If an additional fault is found to exist, one must repeat testing after corrective action is completed to ensure that still another fault has not been introduced.

CONCLUSION

A step-by-step procedure has been discussed here to define the problem, select or eliminate hardware or software as a cause, narrow down the fault, and ensure that all faults have been eliminated. One must exercise judgment during the process and weigh the evidence in order to select the next logical step toward locating the fault. Such a technique is superior to the random fault localization so often practiced.

REFERENCES

Corson, Don: "Solving Elusive Glitch Problems," *Electronics Test*, Nov. 1982, p. 62–67.

Runyon, Stan: "Benchtoppers—Both Analog and Digital—Change Their Looks to Solve New Problems," *Electronic Design*, Oct. 11, 1979, pp. 102–106.

Santoni, Andy: "IEEE-488 Instruments," *EDN*, Oct. 28, 1981, pp. 77–94.

Urdaneta, Nelson, and Bruce King: "Debug ATE Systems Rapidly with a Low-Cost Bus Analyzer," *Electronic Design*, June 25, 1981, pp. 111–115.

14

MANAGING, SUPPORTING, AND USING ATE

The introduction of ATE systems into a testing environment will affect a number of departments. Previous chapters have discussed or alluded to some areas that will experience changes. It may be useful to discuss some of them.

IMPACT ON TEST PERSONNEL

Test personnel will probably experience the greatest impact from the introduction of ATE. Test technicians might fear that automation in the test department will cost them their jobs. In some instances, their concern is unjustified because the ATE system will supplement the present manual systems. For systems with large data requirements, an organization may decide to add an ATE system because the manual test sets cannot handle the test. The manual test set may be retained to handle the portions of the test that are unrelated to the flow of data, such as power supply tests and analog I/O tests, or for the troubleshooting of defective UUTs. In such a case, the number of personnel in the organization could increase.

In other cases, however, their fears may be valid. After all, one reason an organization changes to ATE systems is that it may use less-experienced (and therefore less-expensive) operators. As a result, the organization must consider the impact that a change to ATE will have on its people right from the beginning.

If an organization does determine that it will have an excess of test technicians with expertise on the manual systems that will become obsolete, it will have to take some action. Looking at the situation objectively, an organization can do one or more of the following:

1. Plan to lay them off when it phases out the manual test methods. This is an option that few organizations want to choose because of the future effects it could have on employee relations, morale, and union matters (i.e., if there is a union, it could become tougher in its demands; if there is no union, the layoff could precipitate unionization of the employees). In addition, the organization will lose a number of experienced technical personnel who have already become accustomed to the organization's unique policies and way of doing things.

Such a step could become unnecessary, of course, if the organization had enough assignments elsewhere or enough future work to allow it to keep most of its test personnel. If it plans to switch to ATE to handle a marked increase in future production, for example, it may require even more technicians than it now has to handle the increased troubleshooting requirements.

2. Train them on the new ATE systems. Since the organization will require technicians and engineers to maintain the ATE hardware and software, it can train some test personnel to handle those duties. This training can take many forms. An organization can simply encourage the personnel involved to study the required subjects. It could go so far as to provide an in-house training course in ATE principles, followed by factory training on the ATE system it will obtain. At the least, an organization should do the following:
   a. Pay for the tuition and books of personnel who wish to take evening courses in automated testing and software.
   b. Set up at least a few short courses on subjects relating to the ATE the organization will obtain.
   c. Keep its personnel informed of the details of the ATE system it plans to obtain so they can direct their studies in that direction. If the system will use the BASIC language, for example, they could study BASIC rather than some other language that may be more popular.

3. Assign them to other areas. Organizations often require a diversity of technical personnel and will be able to transfer a few test technicians to such areas as ATE support, manufacturing, or quality control. It can better accomplish such a transition if it begins early in the ATE conversion program to cross-train its personnel and transfer them rather than waiting until the ATE arrives.

A well-planned phaseout of manual methods and phase-in of ATE will have less of an impact on test personnel, of course, than a quick changeover after the ATE system arrives. All departments must begin early to study the impact of ATE and make detailed plans that will allow them to retain all personnel. A planning and implementation group could meet from time to time to adjust the plans and the action to be taken.

IMPACT ON QUALITY CONTROL

The quality department will also feel the impact of a conversion to ATE. As with the test department, the quality department's personnel will be affected the most. Its basic operating methods could also be affected, as was discussed in a previous chapter, so it may have to change its procedures and operating manuals.

In order for quality control personnel to retain their usefulness to the organization, they must become familiar with ATE hardware and software and automatic testing methods. Since many of them worked with manual test sets and electronic inspection procedures, the hardware will cause them few problems. They will have to learn software, however, and the operation of each ATE system to which they will be assigned as inspectors. The organization can handle training and assignment of its quality personnel as it does its test personnel.

IMPACT ON ENGINEERS

Engineers generally experience a minimum of impact when an organization switches to ATE. There are a number of reasons for this.

1. A shortage of experienced engineers generally exists in most industries. Many organizations that have laid off such people have had the experience of being unable to hire them back because they had already hired on elsewhere, often in another part of the country. Their unique technical experience was lost to that organization forever. An organization will thus hesitate to get rid of such personnel if it knows it will have to hire inexperienced or unqualified technical personnel in the future.

2. Engineers are accustomed to learning new things. As a result, they will take the transition to ATE systems and software in stride. Given a reasonable period of time, engineers will fit right into the new environment.

3. Engineers generally seek new challenges, which the introduction of ATE would give them. In fact, it could help retain the restless ones who had planned to move on because their jobs had become dull. It could be many years before ATE, with its complex blend of hardware and software, bores them. Many of them will realize they are getting involved in the initial stages of a growing industry and will have better opportunities for growth.

4. The introduction of ATE should have little negative impact on an organization's requirements for engineers. If anything, the requirements should increase slightly to reflect the higher level of technical support required for the hardware and software of the ATE systems.

IMPACT ON MANAGERS

Managers should also experience little impact. The nature of their work requires them to have the ability to manage any group, whether it uses automatic or manual test methods. The impact they will experience will be the result of the effect of the changeover on the people who work for them. In this respect, the changeover could have more of an effect on individual managers than on anyone else.

To minimize the impact on their departments, managers will have the responsibility of planning for the changeover and taking whatever action is necessary to cushion the impact on the department's personnel. In order to accomplish this, managers will have to do the following:

1. Hire or develop the new expertise they will need, from ATE support engineers to programmers. They should make every attempt, of course, to develop the expertise among the people who presently work in the department or from other departments in the organization. A training program should begin as early in the planning stages as possible, preferably soon after a decision is made to change over to ATE. The training program will have a minimal impact on present production if it is organized well and begins early.

2. Prepare new procedures for implementation as the ATE systems are placed online. Quality control procedures were already discussed. The present documentation procedures may have to expand to include ATE software. If the ATE system will mean a significant increase in production, managers will have to establish more efficient methods of handling the increased work flow.

3. Assure that their people make the transition with a minimum of trauma. Managers must let their people know what effect the transition will have on their jobs. If test technicians will now have to handle more repairs, they should be informed early so they can refresh themselves on troubleshooting techniques.

IMPACT ON TEST-SET SUPPORT PERSONNEL

Groups that support manual test sets will already have much of the hardware expertise they will need to handle ATE systems. They will have to provide training in software, GPIB instruments, and controllers, however, since their personnel might be deficient in these areas. The emphasis in software should be on the languages and any software packages that will be used on the ATE systems that will be obtained.

IMPACT ON OTHER AREAS

Few areas will escape without some change when an organization switches to ATE. Other departments might experience morale problems because their personnel fear that automation will spread to their departments. They must be assured that automatic testing seldom has anything to do with automation of other departments. It would be more likely that other departments would automate first, then the testing department would have to obtain ATE to handle the increased workload.

Other areas will feel the impact in indirect ways. The personnel department may have to search for engineers and managers with new areas of expertise. The technical library will have to order new types of publications. The documentation vaults may have to implement new procedures to handle ATE software and storage media.

Testing departments can be bottlenecks because of the complexity of tests and the scarcity of test sets. The introduction of ATE could speed things up enough that the testing department would cease to be a bottleneck and other areas could become the cause of delays in its place. Pressure would shift to these departments to speed up the product flow.

If overall production increases, departments will have to assure that the work flow increases accordingly. Management will have to develop more efficient methods of moving the product from receiving and production through testing, inspection, and shipping to the customer. An advantage of ATE systems is that they will reduce testing time. If other departments become just as much of a bottleneck as the test department used to be, the ATE investment would have been unwisely made. Management must therefore study the flow of materials and product early in the ATE conversion program in order to be sure that the investment will be worthwhile and in order to investigate areas that can be speeded up.

ATE MANAGEMENT AIDS

A number of methods exist to improve management of a facility with ATE systems. Since the required paperwork can slow down a flow of work, for example, any method that reduces paperwork will improve efficiency.

A bar-code system is an example of a system that can improve efficiency. The use of such a system is illustrated in Fig. 14-1. Upon receipt of a UUT, an operator attaches a bar-code label to the UUT work tag. The operator

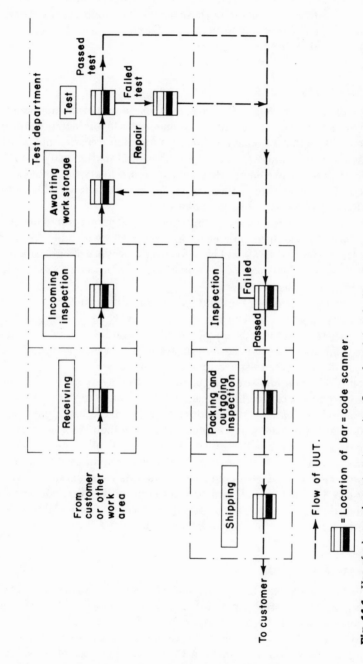

Fig. 14-1 Use of a bar-code system to monitor flow of work in a facility. At points in the flow, the bar code on the UUT is scanned and pertinent information is provided to the system.

214

enters pertinent information into a computer terminal, then scans the bar code with a scanner. The computer associates the bar-code number with the UUT and establishes a record of it.

As the UUT moves through the system, those who handle the UUT scan it with a wand at their work location. This occurs at certain critical points, such as inspection, test, repair, and shipping. They may enter other information concerning the UUT at the same time, much of it through a series of bar codes that are permanent at each station. At the ATE system, for example, permanent bar codes can be placed at the scanner that will indicate to the computer when the operator scans them that the UUT is going into test, test is complete and the unit passed, or the test indicated a failure and the unit is going to repair. The operator would scan the UUT bar code, then whatever permanent bar code applied to the situation.

The computer can keep track of the location and status of the UUT from the time it enters a facility until it leaves. Any customer relations representative, expediter, production control specialist, or manager with access to a terminal can get the status of any UUT within seconds. The computer can also maintain short-term and long-term historical records of each UUT and determine such things as costs, time in work, etc. This ability would reduce the need for much of the paperwork that accompanies UUTs and remains in their permanent record files.

GENRAD TRACS

TRACS (Test and Repair Analysis/Control System) is designed to handle the flow of information in an ATE facility. One configuration of the TRACS system is built around the GenRad 2294 Central Station, a PDP-11/44-based controller. The 2294 contains the central data base for the system. It connects through a network to a number of TRAC terminals installed at various points in the work flow. Each terminal has a bar-code reader and a touch sensitive screen. The operator can select from a menu on the screen by pressing the desired item. Fig. 14-2 and 14-3 show the 2294 and a TRACS repair station.

A number of GenRad ATE systems can interface to the TRACS network. The data base of the 2294 can store the latest test programs for all the UUTs supported and pass them on to a particular ATE system as it requires them. This eliminates the need for a separate disk at each test station.

TRACS will send an alert to designated management terminals when any of the following conditions occur:

1. A particular type of UUT experiences successive failures of the same type.

2. The amount of retesting exceeds an allowable threshold.

Fig. 14-2 The 2294 Central Station and a TRACS terminal. *(Courtesy of GenRad, Inc., Concord, Mass.)*

3. A particular board experiences yields that are lower than the allowable threshold.

The system will keep track of the boards as they move through the system and will give real-time management reports. Afterward, the data that is collected can form the base of historical records.

Fig. 14-3 An operator at a TRACS repair station scanning the bar code on a circuit board. *(Courtesy of GenRad, Inc., Concord, Mass.)*

ATE LONG-TERM SUPPORT

Before the ATE system is placed in operation, management must arrange for its long-term support. This support will have two major goals:

1. Keep the ATE systems operating as much of the time as possible in order to maintain productivity.

2. Maintain and improve the reliability of the ATE system in order to improve product quality.

An efficient ATE support group can keep the ATE system on the air a maximum number of hours a year. This will prevent the test area from becoming a bottleneck or stopping production altogether. A well-run ATE reliability program will also uncover subtle defects in hardware and software and prevent others from occurring during revisions and modifications. As a result, product quality will improve and the product will have less of a chance of being recalled.

In order to realize these goals, management must clearly define responsibilities. In general, responsibilities relating to ATE support will divide among the following groups:

1. Test department, especially the test engineers, technicians, and operators assigned to the ATE systems

2. ATE repair support group, whose technicians repair the ATE systems

3. ATE engineering support department

4. Quality and Reliability Assurance Department

Fig. 14-4 illustrates the division of responsibility in graphical form, while Table 14-1 gives the same information in a more exact format. ATE support is divided into three general areas in the illustrations:

1. Detection of problems and definition of symptoms

2. Troubleshooting and repair

3. Long-term reliability

The first item involves the monitoring of ATE performance in order to detect any problems. Once a problem shows up or is suspected, one must define the symptoms well enough that the complaint can be investigated. Since the test department uses the ATE systems in its work every day, the major responsibility for these items would naturally fall on the test engineers, technicians, and operators. They will probably be the first ones to

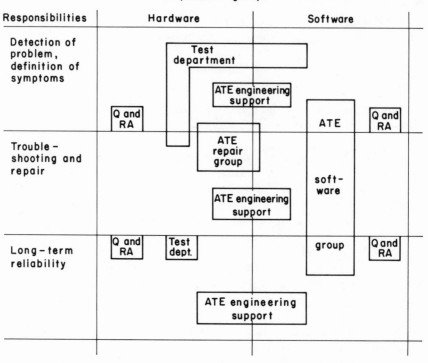

Fig. 14-4 Example of division of responsibility in an organization. The size of a department's block in an area gives a rough indication of its degree of responsibility.

develop a suspicion based on some test result or an analysis of the UUT requirements. They would thus be the logical ones to report their suspicions to the ATE support engineer assigned to that ATE system for investigation. If the ATE system experienced a failure, they would also be the most affected, since testing would stop, and would be the group that would best explain the complaint to the ATE repair support group.

Other groups also share some responsibility for detecting subtle ATE defects. If ATE support technicians notice anything suspicious during repair of an ATE system, for example, they should report it if it is beyond their capabilities to correct. ATE support engineering should also try to weed out ATE defects. Quality and reliability assurance personnel should monitor tests and ATE performance in order to uncover those defects that affect product quality.

The next responsibility—troubleshooting and repair—falls mainly on the ATE repair support group, at least for hardware defects. In many organizations, in fact, tradition or union rules dictate that technicians do all hands-on hardware work of a nonengineering nature. The ATE support engineer

Table 14-1 Ate Support Responsibilities

Responsible group	Detect problems and define symptoms		Troubleshooting and repair		Reliability	
	Software	*Hardware*	*Software*	*Hardware*	*Software*	*Hardware*
Test department	M	M	A	A	M	M
ATE repair group	S	S	M	M	S	S
ATE software group	M	S	M	A	M	A
ATE engineering support dept.	S	S	S	S	M	M
Quality and reliability assurance	S	S	A	A	M	M

Note: M = major responsibility; S = some responsibility; A = minimal responsibility—mainly assistance

will have to provide assistance if the problem is a complex one or it requires an engineering solution, such as the redesign of a circuit or an investigation to locate a subtle ATE defect. For software defects, the ATE support engineer or the ATE software group will handle the correction.

The third item—long-term reliability—is a multifaceted responsibility. It involves such tasks as the following:

1. Maintaining the configuration of the ATE hardware and software. This task will require that ATE systems be up to date and in total conformance with the latest revisions.

2. Ensure that modifications and revisions are correct and implemented without error.

3. Review hardware and software configurations when the opportunity arises in order to uncover subtle defects.

4. Improve such procedures as calibration and self-test programs in order to improve ATE reliability.

The responsibility for these items falls on many of those involved with ATE systems. An organization must give personnel working in ATE engineering support, quality and reliability assurance, and testing the task of assuring that the ATE systems for which they are responsible are free of defects.

THE FUTURE OF ATE

The design, use, maintenance, and management of ATE systems is a complex subject, and this book has attempted to cover them all to some depth. The subject will become even more vast and complex in the future. Advances in robotics, components, computers, and artificial intelligence could bring about another revolution in testing, similar to the one ATE brought about soon after its introduction so few years ago. The dawn of this new era in testing will probably arrive sooner than even the optimists predict.

REFERENCES

Allard, Arthur J.: "Offloading In-Circuit Testers," *Electronics Test*, Nov. 1982, pp. 70–79.

Brian, William J.: "System Manager Enhances LSI Production Testing," *Electronic Design*, Oct. 28, 1982, pp. 119–123.

Chasse, Norm: "Investing in Testing . . . Expanded Production Pays Off," *Circuits Manufacturing*, Dec. 1981.

Faran, James J.: "Computer Program Discloses the Best Board-Test Sequence," *Electronic Design*, Oct. 11, 1981, pp. 169–172.

How to Specify and Justify A.T.E., Application Note 107, Computer Automation, Inc., Irvine, Calif.

Krause, Robert, and Nathan Walker: "Solve Data-Entry Productivity Problems with Bar Codes," *Electronic Design*, Oct. 15, 1981, pp. 207–216.

Weisberg, Martin J.: "Production-Phase Testing Increases Product Throughput," *EDN*, Mar. 20, 1980, pp. 195–202.

———: "Study the Life Cycle to Uncover Complex Test Problems," *EDN*, Mar. 20, 1980, pp. 177–183.

IEEE-488 Subset Capabilities

The following is a list of IEEE-488 Subsets. For a more detailed discussion, one should consult the IEEE-488 standard.

Source Handshake

SH0   no capability

SH1   complete capability

Acceptor Handshake

AH0   no capability

AH1   complete capability

Talker

	Basic Talker	Serial Poll	Talk Only Mode	Unaddress if MLA
T0	N	N	N	N
T1	Y	Y	Y	N
T2	Y	Y	N	N
T3	Y	N	Y	N
T4	Y	N	N	N
T5	Y	Y	Y	Y
T6	Y	Y	N	Y
T7	Y	N	Y	Y
T8	Y	N	N	Y

Extended Talker

	Basic Extended Talker	Serial Poll	Talk Only Mode	Unaddress if MSA LPSA
TE0	N	N	N	N
TE1	Y	Y	Y	N
TE2	Y	Y	N	N
TE3	Y	N	Y	N
TE4	Y	N	N	N
TE5	Y	Y	Y	Y
TE6	Y	Y	N	Y
TE7	Y	N	Y	Y
TE8	Y	N	N	Y

Listener

	Basic Listener	Listen Only Mode	Unaddress if MTA'
L0	N	N	N
L1	Y	Y	N
L2	Y	N	N
L3	Y	Y	Y
L4	Y	N	Y

Extended Listener

	Basic Extended Listener	Listen Only Mode	Unaddress if MSA TPSA
LE0	N	N	N
LE1	Y	Y	N
LE2	Y	N	N
LE3	Y	Y	Y
LE4	Y	N	Y

Service Request

SR0	no capability
SR1	complete capability

Remote Local

RL0	no capability
RL1	complete capability
RL2	no local lock out

Parallel Poll

PP0	no capability
PP1	remote configuration
PP2	local configuration

Device Clear

DC0	no capability
DC1	complete capability
DC2	omit selective device clear

Device Trigger

DT0	no capability
DT1	complete capability

Controller

	System Controller	Send IFC and take charge	Send REN	Respond to SQR
C0	N	N	N	N
C1	Y	—	—	—
C2	—	Y	—	—
C3	—	—	Y	—
C4	—	—	—	Y
C5–C28	—	—	—	—

	Send I.F. Message	Receive Control	Pass Control	Pass Control to Self
C0	N	N	N	N
C1	—	—	—	—
C2	—	—	—	—
C3	—	—	—	—
C4	—	—	—	—
C5	Y	Y	Y	Y
C6	Y	Y	Y	Y
C7	Y	Y	Y	Y
C8	Y	Y	Y	Y
C9	Y	Y	Y	N
C10	Y	Y	Y	N
C11	Y	Y	Y	N
C12	Y	Y	Y	N
C13	Y	Y	N	N
C14	Y	Y	N	N
C15	Y	Y	N	N
C16	Y	Y	N	N
C17	Y	N	Y	Y
C18	Y	N	Y	Y
C19	Y	N	Y	Y
C20	Y	N	Y	Y
C21	Y	N	Y	N
C22	Y	N	Y	N
C23	Y	N	Y	N
C24	Y	N	Y	N
C25	Y	N	N	N
C26	Y	N	N	N
'C27	Y	N	N	N
C28	Y	N	N	N

Controller

	Parallel Poll	Take control synchronously
C0	N	N
C1	—	—
C2	—	—
C3	—	—
C4	—	—
C5	Y	Y
C6	Y	N
C7	N	Y
C8	N	N
C9	Y	Y
C10	Y	N
C11	N	Y
C12	N	N
C13	Y	Y
C14	Y	N
C15	N	Y
C16	N	N
C17	Y	Y
C18	Y	N
C19	N	Y
C20	N	N
C21	Y	Y
C22	Y	N
C23	N	Y
C24	N	N
C25	Y	Y
C26	Y	N
C27	N	Y
C28	N	N

Appendix B

ASCII & IEEE (GPIB) Code Chart

B7 B6 B5 BITS	Ø Ø Ø	Ø Ø 1	Ø 1 Ø	Ø 1 1	1 Ø Ø	1 Ø 1	1 1 Ø	1 1 1
B4 B3 B2 B1	CONTROL		NUMBERS SYMBOLS		UPPER CASE		LOWER CASE	
Ø Ø Ø Ø	0 NUL 0 0	20 DLE 10 16	40 SP 20 32	60 0 30 48	100 @ 40 64	120 P 50 80	140 ` 60 96	160 p 70 112
Ø Ø Ø 1	1 GTL SOH 1 1	21 LLO DC1 11 17	41 ! 21 33	61 1 31 49	101 A 41 65	121 Q 51 81	141 a 61 97	161 q 71 113
Ø Ø 1 Ø	2 STX 2 2	22 DC2 12 18	42 " 22 34	62 2 32 50	102 B 42 66	122 R 52 82	142 b 62 98	162 r 72 114
Ø Ø 1 1	3 ETX 3 3	23 DC3 13 19	43 # 23 35	63 3 33 51	103 C 43 67	123 S 53 83	143 c 63 99	163 s 73 115
Ø 1 Ø Ø	4 SDC EOT 4 4	24 DCL DC4 14 20	44 $ 24 36	64 4 34 52	104 D 44 68	124 T 54 84	144 d 64 100	164 t 74 116
Ø 1 Ø 1	5 PPC ENQ 5 5	25 PPU NAK 15 21	45 % 25 37	65 5 35 53	105 E 45 69	125 U 55 85	145 e 65 101	165 u 75 117
Ø 1 1 Ø	6 ACK 6 6	26 SYN 16 22	46 & 26 38	66 6 36 54	106 F 46 70	126 V 56 86	146 f 66 102	166 v 76 118
Ø 1 1 1	7 BEL 7 7	27 ETB 17 23	47 ' 27 39	67 7 37 55	107 G 47 71	127 W 57 87	147 g 67 103	167 w 77 119
1 Ø Ø Ø	10 GET BS 8 8	30 SPE CAN 18 24	50 (28 40	70 8 38 56	110 H 48 72	130 X 58 88	150 h 68 104	170 x 78 120
1 Ø Ø 1	11 TCT HT 9 9	31 SPD EM 19 25	51) 29 41	71 9 39 57	111 I 49 73	131 Y 59 89	151 i 69 105	171 y 79 121
1 Ø 1 Ø	12 LF A 10	32 SUB 1A 26	52 * 2A 42	72 : 3A 58	112 J 4A 74	132 Z 5A 90	152 j 6A 106	172 z 7A 122
1 Ø 1 1	13 VT B 11	33 ESC 1B 27	53 + 2B 43	73 ; 3B 59	113 K 4B 75	133 [5B 91	153 k 6B 107	173 { 7B 123
1 1 Ø Ø	14 FF C 12	34 FS 1C 28	54 , 2C 44	74 < 3C 60	114 L 4C 76	134 \ 5C 92	154 l 6C 108	174 ¦ 7C 124
1 1 Ø 1	15 CR D 13	35 GS 1D 29	55 – 2D 45	75 = 3D 61	115 M 4D 77	135] 5D 93	155 m 6D 109	175 } 7D 125
1 1 1 Ø	16 SO E 14	36 RS 1E 30	56 . 2E 46	76 > 3E 62	116 N 4E 78	136 ^ 5E 94	156 n 6E 110	176 ~ 7E 126
1 1 1 1	17 SI F 15	37 US 1F 31	57 / 2F 47	77 UNL ? 3F 63	117 O 4F 79	137 UNT _ 5F 95	157 o 6F 111	177 RUBOUT (DEL) 7F 127
	ADDRESSED COMMANDS	UNIVERSAL COMMANDS	LISTEN ADDRESSES		TALK ADDRESSES		SECONDARY ADDRESSES OR COMMANDS	

KEY

octal	25 PPU	GPIB code
	NAK	ASCII character
hex	15 21	decimal

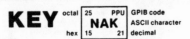

INDEX

ABOUT THE AUTHOR

Allan C. Stover has over twenty years of experience working as an engineer with testing, computers, precision measurement, and automatic test equipment. He is a Senior Engineer in Instrumentation and ATE at Westinghouse Electric Corporation, a Senior Member and Chairman of the Technical Committee on ATE of the Precision Measurements Association, and a Senior Member of IEEE. His text, *You and the Metric System,* was honored as an Outstanding Science Book by the National Science Teachers Association. He is also author of several technical journal articles and papers on ATE and was the Orrin Henry Ingram scholar at Vanderbilt University in 1978 when he received his M.S. degree.